Three Dimensions *of Leadership*

By Olan Hendrix

St. Charles, IL 60174
1-800-253-4276

Published by ChurchSmart Resources

We are an evangelical Christian publisher committed to producing excellent products at affordable prices to help church leaders accomplish effective ministry in the areas of Church planting, Church growth, Church renewal and Leadership development.

For a free catalog of our resources call 1-800-253-4276.

Cover design by: Julie Becker

Manuscript edited by: Dean Richardson

© copyright 2000
    by Olan Hendrix

ISBN#: 1-889638-17-X

Dedication

For
Elizabeth

Three Dimensions *of Leadership*

Contents

Foreword
    John Maxwell 9
Ted Engstrom 11

Preface 13

Chapter 1 – **A Biblical Perspective** 15
    The Bible is Not a Management Text
    All Truth is God's Truth
    Bible Examples
        Joseph
        Moses
        Nehemiah
        Paul
        The Apostolate

Chapter 2 – **The Evolution of Management Theory** 19
    Theories of Management
    Servant Leadership

Chapter 3 – **Management:
Achieving Results Through Others** 25
    Three Models of Management
        Louis A. Allen
        Koontz & O'Donnel
        R. Alec MacKenzie

Chapter 4 – **Leadership vs. Management:
When Definitions Collide** 31
    Leadership: A Transferable Skill
    Management: Understood and Misunderstood

Chapter 5 – **Management: Skills and Tools That Can Be Learned and Acquired** 35
   Definition
   Theology
   Know the Differences!

Chapter 6 – **Ten Leadership Discoveries** 39
   One-on-One
   No Surprises
   Ends vs. Means
   Group Dynamics
   Boards Govern; Staff Manages
   Delegation's Hindrance
   Communication
   Goals
   Leaders are Readers
   Your Time

Chapter 7 – **Planning** 47
   Definitions
   Planning is Difficult
   Decisions Made in Advance
   The Behavior of People
   The Role of Change
   Why We do not Plan
   Principles

Chapter 8 – **Objectives, Goals and Targets** 55
   "Sel not Spel"
   Case Study
   From Absolutes to Methods
   Objectives Made Valid
   Basic Organizational Orientations
   20 Common Errors in Goal-Setting

Chapter 9 – **Organizing** 65
   Ten Commandments of Organization
   Church Order
   Organizational Functional Errors
   Organizational Dynamics
   Centric vs. Radic Groups
   Principles

Chapter 10 – **Job Descriptions** 71
    Three Universal Questions
    Tool, not Document
    Results of Job Descriptions
    The Big Question
    Who Writes the Description?
    Abuses to be Avoided
    A Suggested Format
    Principles

Chapter 11 – **Delegation** 79
    An Overview
    Not All of Your Problems are Spiritual
    Three Essentials of Delegation
    Barriers to Delegation
    The Authority to Delegate
    How to Delegate
    Principles

Chapter 12 – **Development** 89
    The Right Attitude Toward Development
    Three Tasks of Development: Win, Keep, Lift
    Friends, not just Funds
    Development Work is Ministry!
    Development Defined
    Six Components of Development
    Why People Give
    To Ask or Not to Ask
    The Integrated Financial Development System
    The Case Statement
    The Segmented Managed Mailing List
    Marketing/Master Publications Schedule
    Current Giving Program
    Multi-Year Sustained Program
    Capital Campaign
    Planned and Deferred Gifts
    Who's in Charge of Fund Raising

Chapter 13 – **Development and the Local Church** **119**
    Differences
    Teaching Verus Value-Matching
    Annual Emphasis and Pledging
    Welcoming New Donors
    Reporting
    Planned and Deferred Giving
    Never-ending Capital Campaigns
    Endowments

Chapter 14 – **Governance/Boardsmanship** **125**
    There is Hope for Boards
    Sorting out the Roles of Board and Staff
    Why Boards Can't Plan
    A New Design for Committees
    The CEO Job Description
    The Perils of Executive Appraisal
    Boards and Fund Raising

Bibliography **147**

Index

Foreword

By John Maxwell

Olan Hendrix was the first person to teach me Christian management and leadership principles. I still have my notes from attending a management seminar he held in Akron, Ohio in 1975. From that time on I have read everything that Olan Hendrix writes. This book, *Three Dimensions of Leadership*, is a must for those who desire to be effective for God.

Dr. John Maxwell
Founder
INJOY, Inc.

Foreword

By Ted Engstrom

Olan Hendrix is not only a superb teacher of Christian, biblical management principles, but he has been an experienced practitioner as well. The lessons to be learned in how to manage people, as well as programs, are effectively, spiritually, and meaningfully shared in *The Three Dimensions of Leadership* and will be of immense help both to the novice in the exciting field of Christian management and to the veteran administrator.

After having spent an adult lifetime in Christian leadership roles, I find myself challenged and intrigued by the way my friend Olan identifies both the pitfalls and the success challenges in this biblical role, which I fully believe is one of the gifts of the Holy Spirit to the church through His servant. Olan Hendrix has also gleaned great insight on managerial/leadership challenges from his years of productive consulting with scores of Christian organizations worldwide. His clear writing style makes for pleasant and enjoyable reading as well as helpfully sharing his workable guidelines in management.

Hendrix suggests, wisely, that good managers know that they have numerous commitments: commitments to themselves, to their subordinates, to their peers, and to their superiors. Obviously, the Christian manager sees all four of these commitments under the lordship of Jesus Christ. One's ability to recognize these four types of commitments and to manage them is what differentiates the experienced manager from the inexperienced manager.

Good managers know that it's seldom possible for a manager or the people working for him or her to fully understand all of the implications of their failing to meet their commitments. As Hendrix suggests, it is easy for the individual to become so concerned with his own situation that he abandons or modifies his original commitments for others he feels are more important. The ramifications of this failure can ripple through an entire organization. "For want of a nail a shoe was lost; for want of a shoe the horse was lost..."

A Christian organization is one that sees its ultimate purpose as giving glory to God through serving Christ. Good managers in Christian organizations know two more things:

- First, they know there is a creative tension between depending upon God and depending on oneself; between following well-laid plans and following the leading of the Holy Spirit. This tension is never resolved, nor should it be. We are dealing with something much greater than ourselves.

- Second, as Hendrix suggests, good managers in Christian organizations have a quiet confidence that, regardless of what happens, however great the success or dismal the failure, God is at work to do His will. He is the One who is for us.

A wise, widely recognized Christian executive, Max DePree, Chairman of the Board of Herman Miller Furniture Company, has said, "The ultimate test of any administrator is the legacy he leaves to his heir." Olan Hendrix helps us to focus on that legacy. Each of us is responsible for what we leave behind.

Dr. Ted W. Engstrom
President Emeritus
World Vision, Inc.

Preface

In the early days of my ministry I had, perhaps almost unconsciously, come to the conclusion that all of my problems as a servant of Christ were spiritual in nature. It was a stark but liberating discovery to find this not to be true at all. While there are many issues that confront the leader of any Christian organization, I have concluded that the three categories of issues that are most persistent and perplexing have to do with governance, management/leadership and funding.

The following pages are offered as a primer for the conscientious servant of Christ who would seek to experience maximum effectiveness in this complex world in which we serve. A sophisticated and well-read individual will probably not find much help in these pages. However, in my consulting over the years I have discovered that there are many pastors and leaders of para-church organizations who have very limited exposure to these three topics. Therefore, I offer the following pages as an elementary and basic source of information for those who might find help therein.

It is always helpful for me as a reader to know something about the background of the writer to better enable me to understand his points of view. Therefore, I offer the following biographical sketch so you can understand the road that I have traveled thus far in my quest as a servant of the Lord Christ.

After my training at Tennessee Temple University, Temple Baptist Theological Seminary, The Kings College, and the University of Delaware, I began my ministry by founding the First Baptist Church of Elkton, Maryland. From there I went to be the Senior Pastor of Hilltown Baptist Church in Bucks County, Pennsylvania. Hilltown Baptist Church was founded in 1767. I was the twenty sixth pastor, beginning my six years of ministry in 1953. Following this I began my missionary career as US Director for Far Eastern Gospel Crusade, now called SEND, International. Then came a stint as General

Director of the American Sunday School Union, now known as American Missionary Fellowship, in Philadelphia. Later I served as publisher of Regal Books in Ventura, California, was the founding President of the Evangelical Council for Financial Accountability (ECFA), returned to SEND, International for another short stint, and served at World Vision with Ted Engstrom as Director of Leadership Development.

At last count my lecturing, consulting, and preaching had taken me to actually work in eighty-two countries.

As I approach the half-century mark of ministry, I long to know what Hudson Taylor referred to so often in his writings as "greater usefulness to God." My prayer is that the following pages may help you, in ever so small a way, to serve Him well.

Olan Hendrix
Columbus, Ohio

CHAPTER 1

A Biblical Perspective

"Christian leadership represents action, but it is also a set of tools for spiritual men and women. It is not moral or immoral — it is amoral (neither right nor wrong). The issue is the spirituality of the person and how he can better use leadership tools for the glory of God. I believe that every basic, honorable principle in leadership and management has its root and foundation in the Word of God."

—Ted Engstrom[1]

The Bible Is Not a Management Text

When God first sought to reveal Himself to His creation, He utilized what the theologians through the centuries have referred to as "the miracle of all miracles": God became man. Jesus was to eventually exclaim, "He that has seen me has seen the Father." Then, to supplement the grand miracle, God set about to reveal Himself in, of all things, a book—the Bible—the Word of God. When the Scriptures are seen in this light, it has always seemed to me to be ludicrous to reduce them to a management text. The Bible is infinitely more than a mere management text.

The Bible is replete with instances of leadership by men and women of God that provide helpful guidelines and instruction for us today.

All Truth Is God's Truth

Often when I have been lecturing on management topics, people have asked if I could cite chapter and verse to back up what I had been saying. I'm never quite sure how to respond to that kind of question. I think what these inquirers are looking for is a kind of proof text.

Some years ago, I came upon a 200-page, home-produced manual on the subject of leadership, written by one who was clearly a conscientious Christian. He dealt with the traditional topics of management and leadership, and at the end of each presentation he would include a series of Bible references. Needless to say, most of them were far-fetched and bordered on exegetical irresponsibility.

To be sure, biblical examples of management theory can be helpful to the sincere Christian. However, to insist upon a Bible verse for every concept is grossly irresponsible. It is quite common to find authors making snide remarks about management in their attempt to emphasize the deeply spiritual aspects of ministry. Also, it is not unusual to find writers lamenting what they call "the importing of management ideas from secular business into the church." Truth is truth, no matter its origin. Indeed, all truth is God's truth.

There are many beautiful examples of leadership and management in the Scriptures. Here is a quick rundown of the Old Testament leaders' Hall of Fame:

- Nehemiah is a classic example from the Old Testament. Nehemiah displayed great concern for other people, drew upon strength and resources outside of himself, built an effective organizational structure, was passionately goal-oriented, resisted all efforts to deter him from his task, and persevered to the end. By the way, many years ago, my friend, Chuck Swindoll wrote a brief commentary on Nehemiah which he called, *Hand Me Another Brick*. It has enjoyed many printings and to this day provides helpful insight as to how God used Nehemiah.

- Joshua was first a follower, benefiting from having Moses as his mentor; he refused to be a defeatist or pessimist; he relied on the power of God to accomplish the near-impossible.

- Some writers have referred to Moses as the greatest leader that ever lived. Moses made mistakes, grappled with his temptations, persisted until he outgrew his weaknesses, learned self-mastery, and eventually used his authority and power in a responsible manner.

- David was a vulnerable leader, inspired affection, was sympathetic toward the problems of others, refused vindictiveness when it could easily have been rationalized, and was a man after God's own heart.

- Daniel was a man of unusual discernment and good judgment. He worshiped God in private and served him in public. He refused to compromise, could not be bought, was willing to stand alone as a man of faith and principle. Daniel was decisive.

- Samson was very human, and although he failed in careless conduct, he proved God's forgiveness, made a comeback, and learned to accurately identify the true source of his strength, almighty God.

- Joseph, one of the most instructive of Old Testament examples for me, was a man of good judgment, intelligent, hardworking, and exemplary as an organizer.

In the New Testament there are cases of leadership/management that have inspired church leaders through the centuries, including Timothy, John the Baptist, Simon Peter, the apostle Paul, and of course, the glorious example of our Lord Jesus Christ Himself.

In the early days of my wrestling with the subject of management and the Christian organization, I came upon a volume by the Scottish theologian, A. B. Bruce. Of all of the books that I have read on management/leadership through the years, *The Training of the Twelve* has undoubtedly been the most influential single volume I can remember. The magnificent examples of the relationship of the Lord

Jesus to the Twelve has been a constant inspiration to me as I have sought to find ways to get work done through other people.

The Bible is our only source for faith and doctrine but not the only source for management information. While we must not limit our search for management help to the Bible, we should carefully avoid concepts that are unbiblical.

CHAPTER 2

The Evolution of Management Theory

"Management as a practice is very old. But as a discipline, management is barely fifty years old."

—Peter Drucker

Theories of Management

The scientific management theory arose in part from the need to increase productivity. This theory was formulated by Frederick W. Taylor and others in the period from 1890 to approximately 1930. The scientific management theory produced an atmosphere in which finished products could be turned out at the end of an assembly line faster than ever imagined. However, there were serious limitations to this theory. The scientific model held that people were rational and motivated primarily to satisfy their economic and physical needs. This model overlooked the human desire for job satisfaction and the social needs that individuals face.

Next came the classical organization theory spawned primarily by Henri Fayol. He was the first to thoroughly investigate managerial behavior and to systematize his theories.

Then came the transitional theories epitomized by Mary Parker Follett and Chester Barnard. Follett and Barnard built on the classical theories but added new elements, especially in the area of human relations and organizational structure.

The behavioral school of management followed with an emphasis on the "people side" of organizations. This movement was epitomized by what has come to be known as the Hawthorne experiment. Performed at Western Electric's Hawthorne plant near Chicago, the researchers concluded that employees would work harder if they believed management was concerned about their welfare and supervisors paid special attention to them. This phenomenon, subsequently called the Hawthorne effect, has remained quite controversial to this day.

Then came the neo-human relations movement epitomized by Burns and Stalker's declaration, "The beginning of administrative wisdom is the awareness that there is no optimum type of management system."[1] Subsequently W. Edwards Deming, Tom Peters, and many others combined scientific studies and clinical experience to devise a comprehensive and practical set of principles of management, much as others did in the early part of the century. These principles focus on the concept of *quality* in work and on individual workers' relationships with others.

If writers like Drucker, Peters, and others are correct, the new emphasis on human relations management is an important step in the evolution of management thought, one that must be acknowledged in any integrated approach to management theory.

Servant Leadership

The traditional theory of management that began with Plato and moved through the writing of Frederick Winslow Taylor generally reflected the pyramid structure of organizations. In recent years this has given way to a new model, epitomized in the writings of Robert Greenleaf—the theory of servant leadership. In the traditional theory there was a distinct right/wrong polarity; great emphasis was placed upon control. This leadership style expressed itself as a "top down" model, creating great compliance and dependency in followers. The Greenleaf model sought to bring order without traditional control systems and great accountability without control.

Usually the ideas embodied in the terms *servant* and *leader* cause us to conceive of them as opposites. Greenleaf sought to bring together these two words, resulting in a different idea, although a paradoxical one. Greenleaf first coined the expression "servant leadership" in 1970 in an essay titled *The Servant as Leader*.

Born in Terre Haute, Indiana, Robert Greenleaf spent the bulk of his career with AT&T. His second career as creative consultant lasted for 25 years until his death in 1990. His discovery of the concept of the servant as leader came about in 1960 while reading Herman Hesse's *Journey to the East*. Hesse's novel is a mythical account of a group of people on a spiritual journey. The principal figure of Hess's novel is a man called Leo who accompanies the party as a servant, but who sustains the group by his caring spirit in the midst of difficulties. Upon Leo's disappearance, the group falls into disarray and the journey is discontinued. Years later the storyteller discovers Leo and is taken into his religious order that had sponsored the journey. It is only then that he discovers that Leo, whom he had known as a servant, is the distinguished head of that order.

This story gives rise to Greenleaf's conclusion that great leaders must first serve others. Throughout his second career, he was able to confirm and further articulate his thesis that true leadership only comes from an individual whose primary desire is to help others.

Greenleaf wrote in *Servant Leadership*, "It begins with a natural feeling that one wants to serve, to serve *first*. Then conscious choice brings one to aspire to lead....The difference manifests itself in the care taken by the servant — first to make sure that other people's highest priority needs are being served. The best test, and most difficult to administer, is: Do those served grow as persons? Do they, *while being served*, become healthier, wiser, freer, more autonomous, more likely themselves to become servants?"[2]

The *Indianapolis Business Journal* said, "Servant leadership has emerged as one of the dominant philosophies being discussed in the world today."

Robert Greenleaf was impressed by a story told by Ralph Waldo Emerson: "One day he and his son were trying to get a balky calf into the barn; one in the front pulling on a halter and the other pushing from behind. A servant girl watched with some amusement from the kitchen window. When the Emersons gave up, she came, stuck her finger in the calf's mouth and walked it into the barn." That story led Greenleaf to one of his most helpful comments regarding power in leadership. He said, "Coercive power is useful to stop something or destroy something, but not much constructive can be done with it. Latent coercive power in the hands of government seems to be a stabilizing element in society, but the use of it, even the visible threat of its use, too often is destructive. Persuasion is the better tactic."

The traditional model of organization, usually reflected in a pyramid of boxes representing people and their tasks, bore the brunt of much of Greenleaf's leadership philosophy. He once said, "The idea of hierarchy has been around at least since the time of Moses and is deep in the culture. It probably will be around a while longer. Ultimately, though, it will have to go. Lip service has been given for a long time to the idea that people are the most important asset in some companies. But only recently have companies begun to question the traditional organizational assumptions that do not favor people giving their best effort."

It may have been Greenleaf's Quaker background that caused him to put such a biblical perspective upon people within an organization: "The new ethic, simply but completely stated, will be: the work exists for the person as much as the person exists for the work. This new ethic requires that the growth of those who do the work is the primary aim."

Three of Greenleaf's essays show how comprehensive was his thinking with regard to his theory and its application to organizational life. In "The Servant as Leader" he sought to raise the level of performance of organizations themselves, while in "Trustees as Servants" he wrote to encourage boards to accept a more responsible role, albeit a role completely distinct from management.

Dennis L. Tarr, a student of Greenleaf's theory, observed, "Why should one be a servant leader? What practical application does the concept hold? Let me suggest several ideas:

- It works;

- It reinforces the nature of one's professions and calls upon its more noble instincts;
- It is action-oriented; and
- Servant leadership is a commitment to the celebration of people and their potential."

In 1943, Abraham Maslow set forth his theory of human motivation, which held that work in and of itself could provide people with the fulfillment of basic needs. A decade later, Douglas McGregor posited his Theory Y, whereby he encouraged leaders to view their people as creative and responsible individuals. He postulated in Theory X that the assumptions that were commonly held that human beings dislike hard work and are untrustworthy as fallacies. Soon after that Frederick Herzberg reinforced McGregor's theories with his research. In recent years, individuals including Robert Waterman, Tom Peters, Jane Mouten and Renis Likart have reaffirmed the Herzberg theories.

Even more recently, management theorists including Peter Drucker, Max DePree, and many others from the contemporary scene have further lent credibility to the Herzberg theory.

A great deal of our modern management culture emanates from the rise of the baby boomers to positions of leadership. The babies born between 1946 and 1964 are now exerting much influence on our management/leadership culture. They are, to say the least, a new breed with new depths of thinking about how to get things done through other people. The baby boomers, perhaps more than any generation from the past, look upon the word *boss* as a dirty word. Their quest is for teamsmanship where the leader is first among equals. Geoffrey Bellman said, "People don't want managers anymore, they want leaders. And the leaders they want aren't out of the old kind of paternalistic or autocratic molds."

Greenleaf's servant leadership theory has not gone without serious inquiry from thinking people. There is no question that the philosophy set forth by Greenleaf enhanced people's feeling of self-worth and their rise to greater competency and productivity. However, when distorted it can ignore accountability and the inbred depravity of human beings. Critics have even accused Greenleaf of espousing a philosophy which is much more acceptable to writers and publishers than to managers and leaders.

Max Depree, in his book, *Leadership Jazz*, writes, "Above all, leadership is a position of servanthood. Leadership is a forfeiture of rights."[3] He suggests the following characteristics as primary for those who wish to become successful servant leaders:

- integrity
- vulnerability
- discernment
- awareness of the human spirit
- courage in relationships
- sense of humor
- intellectual energy and curiosity
- respect for the future
- understanding of the past
- predictability
- breadth
- comfort with ambiguity and pressure

One of the most serious tests we face as we seek to incorporate Greenleaf's servant leadership theories is in the problem of transition from a strictly hierarchical pyramid model to teamsmanship, which he so vigorously advocated. Greenleaf said the old model of the pyramid structure would be around long after he was gone. He was right. He is gone and the old ways are still with us. Better ways are yet to be codified.

Misunderstood, servant leadership leads many Christian leaders to distortion and excess that can be disastrous. To lead in the work of Christ we must be servants, to be sure. But that must not make us any less leaders.

CHAPTER 3

Management: Achieving Results Through Others

To define a problem clearly and precisely is to go a long way toward solving it. Likewise, to define management work clearly and comprehensively is to go a long way toward actually learning how to do the work.

Management work is the same for *you* in your organization as it is for the Chief Executive Officer of the world's largest corporation. It differs only in degree and sophistication.

The following three outlines depict the anatomy of management work. They are not intended to be sequential or chronological. In this anatomy, like the biological anatomy, there are both vital and vestigial organs. Some aspects of management work can be omitted with fewer repercussions than others.

Three models of management

I. **THE FUNCTIONS AND ACTIVITIES OF MANAGEMENT**
(From *"The Management Profession,"* by Louis A. Allen, 1964. Used with permission of McGraw-Hill Book Company.)

Allen was the great management researcher and strategist of the mid-twentieth century. His outline of the work of management tends to reveal the subject in a comprehensive way.

Function: **Management Planning** – Throwing a net over tomorrow

Activities: Forecasting – Estimating the future
Establishing objectives – Targets measurable in time and quantity
Programming – Vital steps toward objectives
Scheduling – Applying the clock and calendar to tasks
Budgeting – Allocation of all resources
Establishing procedures – Establishing uniform practices for repetitive work
Developing policies – Answers to questions before asked

Function: **Management Organizing** – Putting people and tasks in a structure

Activities: Developing organization structure – Relationship of people and work
Delegating – Sharing the work
Establishing relationships – Responsible for whom and to whom

Function: **Management Leading** – Causing people to take effective action; influence

Activities: Decision making – Arriving at conclusions and judgments

	Communicating – Creating understanding
	Motivating – Inspiring the whole person
	Selecting people – Assessing strengths and weaknesses
	Developing people – Helping people grow in attitude, skills and knowledge
Function:	**Management Controlling** – Insuring that performance conforms to plan
Activities:	Establishing performance standards – Stating targets clearly
	Performance measuring – Agreed upon process
	Performance evaluating – Arriving at judgments
	Performance correcting – One-on-one coaching

II. **PRINCIPLES OF MANAGEMENT** (From *"Principles of Management: An Analysis of Managerial Functions,"* by Harold Koontz and Cyril O'Donnel, 5th ed., 1972. Used with permission of McGraw-Hill Book Company.)

Harold Koontz and Cyril O'Donnel approached the subject of management from the point of view of the scholar and the classroom. Reading these two men gives you the best management thinking from a theoretical view.

The Basis of Management:
   Nature and purpose of planning
   Patterns of management analysis
   The functions and authority of the manager
   The manager and his environment
   Comparative management

Planning:
   Nature and purpose of planning
   Objectives
   Planning premises
   Decision making
   Strategies and policies
   Making planning effective

Organizing:
   Nature and purpose of organizing
   Span of management
   Basic departmentation
   Assignment of activities

    Line and staff authority relationships
    Service departments
    Decentralization of authority
    Committees
    Making organizing effective

Staffing:
    Nature and purpose of staffing
    Selection of managers
    Appraisal of managers
    Development and training of managers

Directing:
    Nature of directing
    Motivation
    Communication
    Leadership

III. **THE MANAGEMENT PROCESS** (From *"The Management Process In 3-D,"* by R. Alec MacKenzie, Harvard Business Review, 1969.) Alec MacKenzie is the street fighter of these three sources. He tended to see management from the view of the practitioner.

Plan:
    Forecast
    Set objectives
    Develop strategies
    Program
    Budget
    Set procedures
    Develop policies

Organize:
    Establish organization structure
    Delineate relationships
    Create position descriptions
    Establish position qualifications

Staff:
    Select
    Orient
    Train
    Develop

Direct:
- Delegate
- Motivate
- Coordinate
- Manage differences
- Manage change

Control:
- Establish reporting systems
- Develop performance standards
- Measure results
- Take corrective action
- Reward

All of this is simply to restate the fact of the intricate and complicated nature of the subject, and to help us break the subject into workable pieces for learning and implementation. When the process of getting work done through other people falters, look carefully at these three outlines. You are very apt to see the point at which you have stumbled.

CHAPTER 4

Management vs. Leadership: When Definitions Collide

Leadership without management is fluff.
Management without leadership is mechanical.

Leadership Is a Transferable Skill

When Senator Robert Dole announced his candidacy for president of the United States, he said to his constituents, "I'm not afraid to lead, and I know the way." Had that been true, and had he been able to convince the electorate, Bob Dole would have been a rare find indeed!

Leadership, or the lack thereof, has always been the key issue, whether the arena be national and world politics, business, education, labor, the arts, or religion. And it is no less true that probably every era of the Christian church has been characterized, at least by some, as being bereft of leadership.

It has often been said that the church is but one generation from extinction—the point being that personal evangelism is God's appointed remedy. But we could also apply that truism to leadership. Without leadership, the mission of Christ's church on earth will certainly be hampered. There is no argument that Jesus is the Head of His church, the Supreme Commander and Authority. But what about the raising up of qualified, godly leaders which He entrusted to us?

You see, leadership development, whether it is in the local church or para-church ministry, is of supreme importance. Without the conscious development of the next generation of leaders, the enterprise dies! Leadership development, then, must be a top-drawer priority for Christians in all spheres of His work! If world evangelism is the challenge to the church without, then leadership development *must* be one of the primary tasks of the church within.

Unfortunately, many dismiss the subject of Christian leadership with the fatalistic assertion that "leaders are born not made," unwittingly echoing the theory that great leaders are born into their greatness and therefore leadership can never be learned. Nothing could be further from the truth! Of course, this is not to deny that some people have infinitely more leadership potential and opportunities than others do. But the plain truth is that almost everything that enables leaders to lead has been *learned*.

Leadership is terribly elusive but certainly not mysterious. It's both sad and illogical that some will diligently endeavor to learn the skills of public speaking, persuasion, teaching, managing, counseling, and so forth, but dismiss leadership. We invite organizational paralysis when we make leadership so ethereal as to be unapproachable by ordinary servants of Jesus Christ. When our thinking becomes cloudy because of the mythical elevation of the words *leader* and *leadership*, it then becomes impossible for us to think strategically in terms of leadership development.

It is my thesis that leadership skills are indeed transferable. It is not my desire or intention to supplant the leadership development processes of the local church, educational institution, or para-church organization. I truly believe that the leadership skills required to be an effective pastor, president, CEO, executive director, vice-president, or whatever the title or position may be in the ministry of Christ, are attainable—perhaps not easily, but certainly attainable.

A review of the plethora of literature on the subject of leadership reveals at least five theories that have been advanced over the decades. These include:

1. the "Great Man Theory" (leaders are born, not made);
2. the "Trait Theory" (leaders exhibit a distinct set of personality traits);
3. the "Behavioral Theory" (leaders behave in certain ways);
4. the "Situational Theory" (leaders adapt their styles to various situations);
5. the "Change Agent Theory" (leaders are those who create change).

Each of these theories attempts to explain the phenomenon we call leadership. Each carries valid points, examples, and research. But none, in and of itself, is fully adequate. In the final analysis, some combination of all is at work, to varying degrees, in any individual leader and his or her success.

Management: Understood and Misunderstood

A more important current debate revolves around the question of the differences (or similarities) between leadership and management. Older texts consistently use the words *management*, *leadership*, *administration* and *supervision* interchangeably. Indeed, Peter Drucker defines managers as, "Those who give direction to organizations, *provide leadership*, and make decisions about the way the organization will use the resources it has available." In stark contrast, H. Ross Perot, billionaire founder of Electronic Data Systems, offered this insight: "People cannot be managed. Inventories can be managed, but people must be led!"

James Kouzes and Barry Posner, in the widely read 1987 book, *The Leadership Challenge*, came to the conclusion that "if there is a clear distinction between the process of managing and the process of leading, it is in the distinction between getting others to do and getting others to want to do. Managers, we believe, get other people to do, but leaders get other people to want to do."[1] And in a similar vein, John W. Gardner wrote, "Leadership is the process of persuasion or example by which an individual (or leadership team) induces a group to pursue objectives held by the leader or shared by the leader and his or her followers."[2]

As you can see, a very great tension, and therefore, misunderstanding, exists between the definitions and applications of the two words *leadership* and *management*. You may have heard someone say in the past, "He (or she) is an excellent manager, but there is not an element of leadership in him." Is that really possible? And if so, what about the commonly heard reverse, "He may be a great leader, but he sure can't manage"?

The distinction between these two concepts is further widened when the attempt is made to classify their actions in opposition. One Christian newsletter author advanced this comparison:

Leadership	*Management*
■ *is an art*	■ *is a science*
■ *thrives on vision*	■ *thrives on systems*
■ *deals with ideas*	■ *deals with processes*
■ *empowers*	■ *controls*
■ *creates change*	■ *creates order*

While the overall intentions of the newsletter's author were to promote leadership in the local church, he may have inadvertently denigrated the role of management and, perhaps, caused greater confusion about the two words.

CHAPTER 5

Management: Skills and Tools That Can Be Learned and Acquired

"People will do a good job if they are provided with management that leads."

— Warren Bennis & Burt Nanus, Leaders[1]

So where do we go from here? Do we widen the gap or narrow it? D. E. Hoste was once asked how it could be determined whether an individual is a leader. His answer was that you simply look to see if anyone is following him. That kind of humorous definition certainly has an element of truth, but it doesn't help resolve the dilemma at hand. Neither does it address the fact that leadership is a set of skills that can be acquired and tools that can be employed to become better than what we are naturally or instinctively. At the outset of his popular book *Leadership Is an Art* (Dell, 1989), Max DePree writes, "Leadership is an art, something to be learned over time, not simply by reading books. Leadership is more tribal than scientific, more a weaving of relationships than an amassing of information."[2]

Definition

To be sure, the words I use have different meanings to different minds. This only contributes to the confusion. The root origin of the word *lead* is a Latin word meaning, "to go." It denotes travel from one place to another. Leaders can be said to be those who "go first." They are the ones who step out to show others the direction in which to head. They are pioneers. They are people who venture into unexplored territory and uncharted seas. They guide us to new and often unfamiliar destinations. They are ones who take us to places we have never been before.

By etymological comparison, the root origin of the word *manage* is a word meaning, "hand." Managing, therefore, denotes "handling" things. Managers tend to focus on issues of control and maintenance.

Obviously, leadership and management are *not exactly* the same thing! That appears to be borne out—if for no other reason—by the origins of the two words. If the terms were synonymous, we would not be having this discussion. But, on the other hand, my experience would argue that in everyday practice the words are almost indistinguishable.

Theology

Apparently Kenneth Gangel came to this same conclusion in his magnificent work *Feeding and Leading*, because he wrote, "Perhaps the purposes of this book are best served by not making that distinction (leadership vs. administration) too clearly. We must state it, however, and the separation of the first two chapters demonstrates that. But here's the key: we want leaders in Christian organizations to be effective administrators and administrators in Christian organizations to be good leaders. In ministry both are better than either, and both can be taught and trained (as Jesus experienced, which the disciples clearly attest)."[3]

Perhaps one of the most respected and cogent arguments for closing the gap was articulated by Louis A. Allen in his book *Management and Organization*, first published in 1958. In a study that has stood the test of time and is routinely cited in modern management, Allen insisted that leading was simply one of the four ingredients of management, the other three being planning, organizing, and controlling. When seen in this light, leadership becomes more a subset of management skills.

Leadership skills can be faked more easily than management. If a person can talk a good game, he can get by for months or even years. Faking management will catch up with us more quickly.

Know the differences!

Leadership	Management
Influence	Achievement
Vision	Goals
Self-discipline	Delegation
Integrity	Control
Focus	Change
Two-way Communication	Decisions
Clear Values	Compromise

To be sure, leadership is different from management. However, the two overlap to the extent that it is not always easy to tell the difference.

CHAPTER 6

Ten Leadership Discoveries

"Leadership is not optional. It is the ingredient essential to the success of any organization. Take away leadership and confusion replaces vision."

— Charles Swindoll

1. **Almost all true management work is done one-on-one, not in groups.**

   Meetings are the #1 time-waster for most leaders. But we waste more than time when we try to do management work in meetings. We sacrifice effectiveness. If management is the work we do to get work done through other people, we should take great care to ensure that the setting is right.

   Many good things can be accomplished in meetings, but not management work.

   There is an old management adage that says we can delegate only to the extent that we can elicit accountability. This is called span of control. Perhaps it is the desire to widen the *span of control* that makes us keep trying to conduct management work in group settings. We think we can hear from more people, inspire more people and give direction to more people if we do it in groups. The result is the dilution of management, not enhancement.

   Sometimes the real issue here is courage, not time. Sitting face-to-face, one-on-one takes courage. Most of us are much bolder in front of a group than we are face-to-face, with the door shut. This makes us vulnerable. We must be prepared with facts and skills. We can wing it in a group, but not one-on-one.

2. **A cardinal rule of management is to never surprise your followers.**

   Peter Drucker once said that a well-managed organization is dull. He is right! People are at their best in an organization when they know what to expect. They are at their worst when change is thrust upon them suddenly.

   Recognizing this fact many leaders go to the other extreme, asking everybody about everything before even the smallest decision is made. This is just as bad, maybe worse. There is a world of difference between being a leader and being a meeting-convener and consensus-gatherer. Wisdom is required to know the difference.

   The real issues are involvement and trust. People don't need to vote or have everything announced in a staff meeting, but they do need to know they are involved in changes that affect them. People know intuitively when they can trust leaders to care genuinely about what they think.

3. **Evaluate every board meeting discussion with the *ends versus means* distinction.**

   John Carver may have made the greatest contribution ever to boardsmanship when he clearly distinguished *ends* and *means*. He says that boards should be occupied with ends; such as, What good? For whom? At what cost? Staff should create and implement means; such as, programs, activities, and so forth.

Failure to clearly distinguish between the two can be dangerous for any organization. Board members become disillusioned with trivia and quit. The staff becomes frustrated with micromanagement by the board.

One board member complained that board meetings he had attended consisted of nothing but budgets, buildings, and baloney!

There is a valuable barometer to help with this problem. Take out the minutes of your last several board meetings. Look at each item. If your organization is like most, 90% of the items are *means* rather than *ends*. This indicates that a storm is on its way, if it has not already arrived!

Boards can govern, with care and discipline, but they can never manage. More about this in a later chapter.

4. Understand and abide by the facts of group dynamics.

People do and say things in groups that they would never do or say in a private conversation. I first encountered this fact as a young pastor in my first church. Having a congregational form of government, we held many business meetings, too many business meetings. I was appalled at how all of us had the potential to change personalities during meetings when we were discussing difficult issues about which we felt strongly.

It took many years for me to discover workable strategies for group meetings. I could have been more effective as a servant of my people had I known the following two strategies. They are both unbelievably simple and universally usable.

The first strategy is to *identify the opinion leaders of the group* with regard to the change you seek to introduce, and then talk with each one privately. Once you have broached the subject, the trick is to ask open ended questions and then listen. The purpose for meeting with the individual is not to convince him or her of anything but to get him or her to tell you honestly and freely how they feel about the matter. In some instances these private conversations will lead you to delay or even abandon the subject. As disappointing as this may be, it will save you from a showdown in a group setting.

The second strategy I learned much too late is to *structure meetings so that difficult subjects can be discussed without an explosion*. This is done very simply by removing the decision from the discussion. The chair simply states that a certain topic is to be taken up and a specific amount of time will be devoted to the topic but that no decision will be made. When the time has expired, the discussion ends. Then, with the concurrence of the leaders, the subject can be put on the agenda for a decision at a future meeting. This maximizes the light and minimizes the heat!

5. Boards should govern; staff should manage.

I once knew an organization that called its governing body the board of managers. And indeed they tried to be managers. They met every Friday at noon, devoting hours to trivia within the organization.

A group of people meeting occasionally has some chance of succeeding in governance but no chance of doing management work.

Definitions might help here. Governance is the work done by a group of people establishing *ends* for which the organization exists and then ensuring accomplishment by predetermined systems of monitoring. On the other hand, management is the creation and implementation of *means* for the achieving of the *ends* for which the organization exists. Confuse the two and you dilute both. The inevitable result is that the board blames the staff for lack of accomplishment and the staff blames the board for not doing its job.

Ideally, the board has nothing to do with *means* except to tell the staff plainly what it will not allow. (More about this later.) This frees the board to govern and the staff to manage.

6. The greatest hindrance to delegation is emotional in nature.

Overworked leaders have to find something to blame for their busy schedules. The easiest target is the ineptness of their people. Your people are probably as good as any other group of people. If you blame them then you are off the hook for training and coaching. Some of us are better at bearing up under heavy schedules than bearing the burden of delegation. Few tasks in management are higher risk than delegation.

Delegation is the essence of management work. From the day Moses' father-in-law advised him to divide the work, until the present, thinking people have known they have to do the same. But we still find ways to get around the process. Why is this so universal among leaders? Of course there are skills and techniques we need to learn and apply, but the real hindrance is emotional.

After hearing me give a talk in Japan on delegation, a distraught man asked me, "How can I give over to others the work God has called me to do?" For this man the issue was not skills. The issue was emotional.

There is a world of difference between being one who does work and one who also gets work done through others. The difference is delegation.

Knowing how to delegate is not enough. We also have to be free and mature enough to share both the work and rewards with others. I can teach people the "how" of delegation, but I can't make them mature in their emotions; they have to do that for themselves. I will discuss this important subject in greater detail in chapter 10.

7. Take full responsibility for communication.

There are many burdens that are hidden in the shadows until you are well down the road of leadership. Communication is one of them. In my early days I took great comfort in telling people, "Ah, but you didn't understand me." It was an unpleasant and burdensome discovery to learn that as a leader, I can never afford to say that again. I now know that it is the responsibility of the communicator to make sure there is understanding.

Communication is the process of securing understanding—not necessarily agreement. Most of our problems come from misunderstanding and not from disagreement. Furthermore, the higher the level of understanding the greater the tolerance for disagreement. Realizing this fact alone will make us more willing to bear the load of ensuring comprehension.

The principle here is that the responsibility for securing understanding rests solely with the person initiating the communication.

8. Discover the power of goals.

My friend Ed Dayton said that a goal is an end result measurable in time and quantity. Anything less is a "warm fuzzy." We have all made long lists of warm fuzzies that caused us to feel good for the moment, but imparted no power for achievement.

The simple truth is human beings don't have trouble achieving goals; they only have trouble setting them. Once a target is identified, measurable in time and quantity, achievement is almost assured. Only then are commitment and focused effort possible.

Organizational goals are possible only when the leader is highly goal-oriented personally. The starting point is for the leader to set personal goals and only then begin the work of inspiring followers to pursue group goals.

The single greatest enemy to group goals is activities. Any organization that has been in existence for more than five years runs the risk of having no goals, only activities. I know of a man who had a large sign on the wall of his office where he was forced to look at it all day long. It read: "Is what I am doing or about to do getting us nearer our goals?" Clearly measurable goals enable us to be severely critical of our activities.

Most organizations come into existence with a high goal orientation, then tend to deteriorate to an activity state. Once that has happened it is extremely difficult to recover a goal orientation. In fact, it is often easier to start a new organization than to renew a stagnant one. It is easier to give birth than to raise the dead! This might explain why the entrepreneurial-type person leaves one organization to found another of his own.

Organizational renewal is difficult but possible—but only with a leader at the helm who is obsessed with identifiable, measurable goals that he or she imparts with great power and inspiration.

9. Leaders are readers.

Everything you need to know about how to do your work is hidden somewhere in a book. All the pitfalls you face have been experienced by others and written about sometime, somewhere.

Five years from now you will be the sum total of the books you have read and the people who have influenced you. Choose carefully the material you read and the people with whom you associate.

When God sought to reveal Himself to man He utilized the grand miracle: the Incarnation. Jesus said, "He that has seen Me has seen the Father." Then He supplemented that revelation of Himself with, of all things, a book—the Bible. That alone should make all of us into book lovers, especially of The Book!

The fact is that most of us don't read more simply because we don't read well. To learn to read well, one must learn new skills: reading skills. There are plenty of books and tapes on the subject of rapid-reading skill development. Pay the price in time and discipline to learn how to read well.

However, even people who read well need help in reading as much as they should. Some of the things that help me in my pursuit of this goal include the following:

- *Make* time to read; you will never simply *find* time to read.

- Commandeer any size chunk of time for reading, whether five minutes or an hour. Rarely do busy people find the time to read an entire book in one sitting, but they can complete it by seizing reading time in bits and pieces.

- Keep several books going at all times.

- Read widely, not just books on subjects with which you are already familiar.

Peter Drucker calls people like you and me *knowledge workers*. If he is right—and I am convinced that he is—we must pay the price to become good students.

10. Great leaders are extremists in the use of time.

I delight to tell groups about the busiest man I ever knew. He is my very dear, dear friend, Ted Engstrom. While I have known Ted for 25 years, we became close in a working relationship in the mid '70s when he was chairman and I was president during the founding of the Evangelical Council for Financial Accountability. At the time he was the head of World Vision, an active churchman, father, husband, golfer, prolific author, and member of at least a dozen boards. Yet I never heard him say he was busy or tired, and I never once felt rushed in his presence. Ted, better than anyone I have known, knows how to control his time.

To control days and hours, we must first control minutes. Time gets away from us in small chunks. There are two great and simple strategies for successful time utilization:

1. knowing accurately where your time is going; and

2. learning to say no.

The starting point for most of us is a time log. It is so simple. Keep a record in 15-minute segments of how you are spending your time. It is natural for us to have a distorted view of where our time is being spent. If you are like most, you will find that much of your time goes for meetings, telephone conversations, and interruptions. Once you know where your time is going, then and only then are you in a realistic position to take control and make corrections.

The second strategy is to learn to say "no" in a gracious way to decline requests and invitations. Ray Ortlund, my pastor and dear friend, once told me that he was inundated with requests to speak here and to go there and to do something else. He discovered that it was easier to say "no" later than on the spot. So, when someone made a request of him he would reply that he would consult his date book, think it over and call him or her back with an answer. Good strategy!

CHAPTER 7

PLANNING

"An intelligent plan is the first step to success. The man who plans knows where he's going, knows what progress he is making, and has a pretty good idea when he will arrive. Planning is the open road to your destination. If you don't know where you're going, how can you expect to get there?"

—Basil S. Walsh

"Planning is the mode by which a complex social organism can learn what it seeks to become, perceive how to attempt to do so, test whether the progress has been made, and reevaluate along the way whether the original goal is still desirable."

—Warren Bennis

Informed planning is based upon the fact that phenomena do not occur singly. Everything comes preceded, accompanied, and followed by many other events and issues. The cause-and-effect relationship of events is a powerful natural law. Planning, therefore, is doing specified work today to cause desired results tomorrow.

Louis A. Allen in *The Management Profession* defines planning as "the work a manager performs to predetermine a course of action." According to Allen, the all-encompassing work of planning includes the following:

1. *Forecasting*: Estimate the future.

2. *Establishing Objectives*: Determine the end results to be accomplished.

3. *Programming*: Establish the sequence and priority of action steps to be followed in reaching objectives.

4. *Scheduling*: Establish a time sequence for program steps.

5. *Budgeting*: Allocate resources necessary to accomplish objectives.

6. *Developing Procedures*: Develop and apply standardized methods of performing specific work.

7. *Creating Policies*: Devise and interpret standing decisions that apply to recurrent questions and problems of significance to the enterprise as a whole.

What all this says is that *planning* is one of the most important words in the management vocabulary. Always vital in successful management, planning has assumed unparalleled importance in these days of high-speed, high-tech change.

Abraham Lincoln said in 1858, "If we could first know where we are, and whither we are tending, we could better judge what to do and how to do it."

The single most important aspect of planning is that it should always be done by the people who bear the responsibility for its implementation. I have never known of a planning committee that was effective. The idea that a group of human beings can do planning for an organization when they themselves are not the ones charged with doing the work makes very little sense. Indeed, a group of human beings that is not involved with implementation might serve as a valuable resource to the staff for creativity. However, that group should function in a staff relationship and not in a line relationship.

Definitions

Definitions are extremely important in the quest for conceptualization of abstract truth. Therefore, spend a few minutes with me attempting to define planning.

Roger D. Bourdon said, "Planning is the continuous process of systematically evaluating the nature of the work, defining its long-term objectives, identifying quantifiable goals, developing strategies to reach these objectives or goals and allocating resources to carry out the strategies."

Another effort at defining planning is, "Predetermining today a course of action for tomorrow." Yet another is, "Throwing a net over tomorrow to cause to happen what we choose."

To put it another way, planning is being tomorrow-minded rather than yesterday-minded. Evangelical Christian organizations especially have problems here. So much of what we are is determined by revelation and history that we tend to forget tomorrow in our thinking. Someone quipped that we sometimes appear to be driving into the future looking in the rearview mirror!

Consider planning as decisive—doing work today designed to cause specified occurrences tomorrow.

Planning Is Difficult

Why do we have such difficulty with planning? A vice president of a consumer electronics company said, "Today the world is changing so rapidly that we cannot train to meet a given situation. We must educate people to cope with whatever changes may occur." There are only three things about the future of which we are certain:

1. The future will not be like the past.

2. The future will not be like we think it is going to be.

3. The rate of change will be faster than ever before.

Look again at the components of planning. These tasks fit together like pieces of fine machinery. You may take them out to examine them one at a time, but for a plan or a machine to work, all of the components must fit and work together.

Decisions Made in Advance

With these seven parts of planning in mind (forecasting, establishing objectives, programming, scheduling, budgeting, developing procedures, and creating policies), consider the key traits of planning.

The first trait is that planning consists of decisions made in advance of action. I saw a comic strip some time ago. A fellow was speeding along in his car toward a fork in the road. There was a sign in the island in the middle of the diverging roads that said, "Take either road." The driver crashed into the signpost in the middle. The final panel of the comic strip shows the fellow climbing out of his car, saying to the policeman, "I couldn't make up my mind which one to take."

Planning is difficult because planning requires us to embrace the sometimes intimidating affirmation: "Today we are deciding issues related to the future." Planning involves decisions made in advance of action.

We all know that once an arrow has been aimed at the bull's eye and subsequently released from the bow, it is impossible to intercept and alter the course of the arrow. Actually, I think we would often prefer to be without purpose rather than select a purpose that commits us—our arrow—to a definite direction. Today's purposes, aims and decisions commit us for tomorrow.

The Behavior of People

Another defining characteristic of planning is that it deals with the future behavior of people.

One of the most important lessons we can learn about the future behavior of people is found in a catchy phrase: *Take people action*. We must condition people! Remember that management on the part of the Christian worker is never to engage in subterfuge, insincerity, or anything that is dishonest. Never! Conditioning does not mean deceiving people. Conditioning means giving them information to prepare them for change. It means involving them whenever possible in whatever you know about the situation.

R. E. Thompson, founder of Missionary Internship and missionary to China, says, "Tell your people everything you can tell them and they will seldom demand that you tell them what you should not tell them. There is a place for secrets, but if you will tell your people all you can, you will rarely find them asking to know more."

How you go about telling depends on the subject matter and the situation at hand. Some information can be adequately conveyed in a memorandum or a letter, but letters are poor vehicles for communication. The best way, of course, is face-to-face, one-on-one. Sometimes you will have to resort to group settings. But the larger the group, the less likelihood of securing understanding. Wise leaders will take advantage of every opportunity with people to condition them. (Think of how God revealed His *ways* to Moses and His *acts* to the children of Israel.) The person at the top must be constantly conditioning his people. Take every opportunity to do so.

Timing is critical in planning. A good idea presented prematurely can fall on deaf ears. People who would support you idea tomorrow might reject the plan today.

The Role of Change

A third trait of planning is that it involves change. Change is the most evident characteristic of our time. Former American Management Association (AMA) president Lawrence Appley described rapid change in this way: "We are confronted with the rate of change of change." It is no longer that rate of change, it is the changing of change!

Emerson lamented, "...improved means to unimproved ends." Einstein concurred: "Few things so characterize our days as perfection of means and confusion of goals." The world often improves and perfects the means to uncertain or less-than-noble ends; the church pursues noble ends, but with antiquated means. Leaders must prepare themselves and their followers for change. Not change for the sake of change, but change for the sake of accomplishment.

Why We Do Not Plan

Why do we not make the effort that is required to establish objectives, estimate the future program, and draw up budgets and procedures? What are the barriers to planning? Let me suggest that the first reason is simply that we do not know how. Some of us do not plan because we have never seen it done.

Second, we do not plan because most of us prefer to do things rather than think about them. Planning is thinking. Planning is coordinating. Planning is analyzing. Planning is communicating. Planning is interacting. Planning is revising, appraising, and it is easier to plunge into action than think. One of my clients refers to this as, "Ready, fire, aim."

Third, another formidable barrier to planning is the uncertainty of the future. We do not know what tomorrow is going to be like. This uncertainty must drive us to do the work of planning, not deter us from doing it.

Principles

As we proceed in the actual planning process, there are six principles to be observed.

The principle of present choice teaches us that current decisions limit future action. A missionary in children's work had a classic example of this problem. She was engaged in children's work in Japan. Soon after she became involved in the work she found that many of the children came to meetings with runny noses. So, she would wipe noses. She soon found, however, that much valuable time was spent wiping noses! Finally, she decided, "My goal is not to see that these children have clean noses. My goal, in these limited thirty or forty minutes that I have with these little ones, is to teach them something from the Word of God." So she left their noses alone.

The principle of positive action teaches us that the probability of a future event occurring increases as effort is applied systematically toward its realization.

We must have such a commitment to a goal, and understanding of that goal, that draws together in its completion. We ought to be so fully oriented to the goal that we will critically evaluate other pressing needs and activities before agreeing to them.

I find that most Christian organizations are so diversified in their activities that they are unnecessarily ineffective. We have an exaggerated concept of our abilities and resources, and an undisciplined approach to our task. One mission executive stated the goal for his organization as: "Our goal is to evangelize the whole world." What an inflated concept of his abilities and resources!

The principle of commensurate effort teaches us that effort applied should be commensurate with or proportionate to the results desired.

The principle of planning stability teaches us that the stability of a plan tends to vary inversely with its extension. This means that I can plan very accurately for a week; with less accuracy for a month; and with even less accuracy as the time is extended out further. What does this mean in regard to your planning? Does it mean that because of the instability of the lengthening of the plan, one should not plan? No. It makes planning all the more imperative. Also, it means that a good, long-term plan is continually updated. Planning is a continuing, ongoing work.

The greater the departure of planned changes from present ways, the greater the potential resistance by the people involved. Do you know who resists change? We all do. It is most probably true that the older we are the more we resist change, but not necessarily so.

The more insecure we are, the more we resist change. Provincialism contributes to resistance to change. We have to anticipate this resistance, and we must not scold our people when they resist change. Let us appreciate the facts that we ourselves also oppose change and that we do not welcome having new things imposed upon us. If we realize those facts about ourselves, it will help us understand them in others.

Future events tend to result from current and past occurrences. Organizations are what they have been becoming. We determine our tomorrow to the extent that we identify clearly what we want to accomplish and apply efforts today to bring it to pass. This is present diligence with clearly defined tomorrow-mindedness. Planning is hard work well worth the effort.

CHAPTER 8

Objectives, Goals & Targets

" It's not my job to control the church. It's my job to lead it."

—Rick Warren, pastor,
Saddleback Community Church

My friend Ed Dayton says that objectives are valid only when they are measurable in time and in quantity. He's right! Anything less constitutes mere rhetoric.

Most Christian organizations come into existence because of the vision of an entrepreneurial-type leader. While his vision might not be codified, indeed it might not even be written down, it is infectious to his followers. Once the founding stage of an organization has been established, it almost inevitably moves toward the plateau era and eventual decline. It is rare for the founder of an organization to successfully lead it through the inescapable organizational phases that follow. I once heard a leader of what used to be called the China Inland Mission say that Hudson Taylor, the founder, died just in time to save the organization. Leaders of all organizations, including entrepreneurial-type founders, must continually struggle to recapture organizational goal-orientation.

If your organization has been in existence for more than five years or so, there is every probability that you no longer have any goals whatsoever, just activities and programs. Religious organizations, including evangelical Christian organizations, face a very special set of problems in this area. Profit-generating businesses, which can survive only if there is a good profit margin and satisfied customers, are different from not-for-profits in that for them, losing sight of goals (profits and happy customers) means losing the business. Charitable organizations, however, can go indefinitely, because generally people will continue to give money to them whether pertinent goals are in place or not.

The biggest single enemy of goals is activities. As long as we can keep the activities going, which in turn keeps donor awareness up and hence causes monies to be given, the organization remains in existence whether there are goals being achieved or not.

"Sel not Spel"

I once read an arresting story about a man named Gooch. He was a newly hired traveling salesman who wrote his first report back to the home office. It stunned the brass in the sales department because it was obvious that the new guy was ignorant. Here's what he wrote:

> "I seen this outfit wich they ain't never bot a dimes worth a nuthin from us and I sole them some goods. I'm now agoin to Chicawgo."

Before the sales manager could give the man the heave-ho, along came this letter from Chicago:

"I come hear and sole thum haff a millyon."

Fearful if he did, and even more afraid if he didn't fire the ignorant salesman, the sales manager dumped the problem into the lap of the president. The following morning the ivory-towered sales department members were astonished to see the salesman's two letters posted on the bulletin board, along with this message from the president:

"We ben spendin two much time tryin to spel insted of tryin to sel. Let's watch those sails. I want everybody should reed these here letters from Gooch who is on the rode doin a grate job four us and yew should go out and do like he done."

Obviously, any sales manager would prefer to have a salesperson that can both sell and spell. However, most of the world is so culture-committed that a man will be chosen and hired for his spelling acumen rather than his selling skills, unless great management care is taken!

Goals are dynamic. Nothing releases organizational energy like a goal, nothing generates creativity like goals, and nothing in the natural realm satisfies the heart and mind of man like a goal!

Since you are reading these pages, it could well be that you are the leader of an organization that has stagnated and is in need of organizational renewal. The first step might be for you to become goal-oriented in your own life and behavior. I am often asked to conduct management audits for local churches and other Christian organizations. Frequently I find that the leader is not well disciplined in the utilization of his time. I usually suggest that the very first step the pastor/leader take is to keep a personal time log for two weeks, identifying how his time is used in 15-minute increments. This helps immeasurably to understand accurately where one's time is going. All of us tend to exaggerate how busy we are and we tend to misinterpret how our time is being utilized.

Case Study

You may have heard the story of Charles Schwab and Ivy Lee. Charles Schwab, president of Bethlehem Steel Company, granted an interview to an efficiency expert named Ivy Lee. Lee was telling Mr. Schwab how his firm could help him do a better job of managing the company, when Mr. Schwab broke in to say something about how he wasn't managing as well as he knew how to. Schwab went on to tell Ivy Lee that what was needed wasn't more *knowing*, but a lot more *doing*. He said, "We know what we should be doing; now if you can show us a better way of getting it done, I'll listen—and pay you anything within reason."

Lee said that he could give him something in twenty minutes that would increase his achievements by at least 50%. He handed Charles Schwab a blank sheet of paper and said, "Write down the six most important things you have to do tomorrow." Mr. Schwab did as requested; it took him about three minutes.

Lee then said, "Now, number them in the order of their importance to you and the company." That took about five minutes.

Now Lee said, " Put the paper in your pocket, and the first thing tomorrow morning, take it out and look at item number one. Don't look at the others, just number one. Start working on it and stay with it until it's completed. Take item number two the same way; then number three and so on until you have to quit for the day. Don't worry if you have only finished one or two. You'll be working on the most important ones. The others can wait. If you can't finish them all by this method, you couldn't have finished them by any other method either. And without some system, you'd probably take ten times as long to finish them—and might not even have them in the order of their importance.

"Do this every working day, " Lee went on. "After you've convinced yourself of the value of this system, have your employees try it. Try it as long as you like, and then send me your check for whatever you think the idea is worth."

The entire interview hadn't taken more than a half-hour. In a few weeks Mr. Schwab sent Ivy Lee a check for $25,000 with a letter saying that from a money standpoint the lesson was the most profitable that he had ever learned. It was later said that it was this plan that was responsible for turning what was then a little-known steel company into the biggest independent steel producer in the world. It also helped Charles Schwab make $100 million.

One idea: consider the concept of taking things one at a time, in their proper order, of staying with one task until it's completed before going on to the next. However, the process of leading an organization to become goal-oriented instead of activities-centered is a far more complex undertaking. Many factors enter in:

- What is your relationship to the people in the organization?
- What is the sociological makeup of the organization?
- What kind of governance has the organization been accustomed to?

- How much influence do you really have regarding the organization's goals?

Discovering accurate answers to these kinds of questions must be the first step in bringing about organizational renewal.

From Absolutes to Methods

The evangelical Christian organization is especially susceptible to difficulty when it comes to recreating a goal-orientation. Few tasks are more difficult than recreating organizational goals. This stems, in part, from the fact that we have our theological absolutes brought with us from our past. Thus, there is considerable confusion when it comes to distinguishing between absolutes, purpose, objectives, goals, and methods. The following diagram might help as you attempt to explain these differences to your followers.

Absolutes
(Theological)

Purpose
(Philosophical)

Objectives
(Long-Range Results)

Goals
(Short-Range Results)

Methods
(Activities)

The absolutes are theological, derived from the Word of God, and changes in this category are not even considered.

"Purpose" refers to the philosophical and psychological aspects of what the organization exists to accomplish. Purposes usually have to do with categories that are ongoing and rarely need to be changed.

Objectives are long-range end results, measurable in time and in quantity.

Goals are short-range achievements that are stepping stones toward the achievement of objectives, and they are also measurable in time and in quantity.

Methods are the programs or activities in which the organization engages in hopes of achieving goals, objectives, and purpose, under the umbrella of the absolutes.

It is worth emphasizing here: "Difficulties in mission arise when attachments, proper to doctrine, are transferred uncritically to methods of work." That's exactly correct. Our organizational absolutes ought not even be considered for change. But the difficulty comes when we transfer that element of the permanent to the activities in which we engage. In other words, our activities, especially in evangelical Christian organizations, also tend to become our absolutes.

The failure to distinguish between the categories listed above is the single greatest enemy to effective organizational goal setting.

Let's look at it another way. Objectives become valid and powerful in organizational life to the extent that they are *definitive*, *inspiring*, and *embraced by the group*, and that they *submit to concentration*.

Definitive — The more easily the followership can comprehend goals and objectives, the better. Physical and statistical objectives are easier to comprehend than abstract educational and behavioral ones.

Inspiring — There must be meaningful reasons for pursuing objectives. Don't minimize the importance of the inspirational side of leadership. All of us would like to believe that our followers are primarily rational beings having emotions. I sometimes think we might better be described as emotional creatures occasionally resorting to reason!

Embraced by the group — This is obviously imperative, as every leader knows. The questions becomes, "How do we get followers to accept (or claim) ownership of a set of objectives?" Dictatorial leaders demand allegiance and compliance. The passive leader sits by and waits for ownership to drift upward through the group from the bottom. Leaders who tell their people that something is the will of God for them and they had better do it often use blatantly coercive methods. All of us who have ever attempted to lead people know that there is no great achievement until there is group ownership. How we attempt to bring this about is critical. We must lead without being domineering. We must lead without resorting to questionable methods. We must lead but never manipulate.

An almost universal error that I have observed is the assumption that people have to vote on something in order for them to take ownership of it. Nothing could be further from the truth! People have to *participate* in order to come to genuine and long-lasting ownership, but it is not necessary for them to vote on it. Indeed, many times in my experience people have voted one night on a matter, only to reverse themselves on the matter the following day!

Submit to concentration — Objectives are valid, meaningful, and powerful only to the extent that they enable the group to turn away from some activities and to concentrate on those things that will bring about the desired objective.

Basic Organizational Orientations

The basic orientation of most groups during their formative years is toward objectives and end results. Most organizations come into being with a very clear set of objectives, usually inspired and articulated by an entrepreneurial-type leader. This organizational orientation is continually asking itself, "What are we trying to get done?" Unfortunately this outlook tends to dissipate three to five years after the organization has been founded.

A greater focus on tasks and activities is the next step in the spiral downward in organizational life, even in evangelical Christian organizations brought into existence by prayer and in obedience to the teaching of the Scriptures. The basic question this organization keeps asking itself is, "Are we *doing* things?"

In late-state organizational orientation the basic question the organization asks itself is, "Are we doing things the right way?" This is the bitter dregs of organizational deterioration. Such an organization perpetuates its ineffectiveness because of its preoccupation with polity.

It has been often and correctly observed that people do not have difficulty achieving their goals; they have difficulty setting them. What follows is guidance on what not to do as you begin to map out your personal and organization goals.

20 Common Errors in Goal-Setting

By George S. Odeirne

1. The leader doesn't clarify *common objectives* for the whole group.
2. The leader sets goals too low to challenge the individual subordinate.
3. The leader doesn't use prior results as a basis for using intrinsic creativity to find new and unusual combinations.
4. The leader doesn't clearly shape his unit's common objectives to fit those of the larger unit of which he is part.
5. The leader overloads individuals with patently inappropriate or impossible goals.
6. The leader fails to cluster responsibilities in the most fitting positions.
7. The leader allows two or more individuals to believe themselves responsible for doing exactly the same thing when he knows that having one responsible party is better.
8. The leader stresses methods of working rather than clarifying individuals' areas of responsibility.
9. The leader emphasizes tacitly that pleasing him is what counts rather than achieving the job objective.
10. The leader makes no policies as a guide to action, but waits for results and then issues *ad hoc* judgments in correction.
11. The leader doesn't probe to discover what his subordinate's program for goal achievement will be. He accepts every goal uncritically without a plan for successful achievement.
12. The leader is too reluctant to add his or her own known needs to the program of subordinates.
13. The leader ignores the very real obstacles which will face the subordinate in achieving his goals, including many emergency or routine duties which consume time.
14. The leader ignores the proposed new goals or ideas of subordinates and imposes only those he or she deems suitable.
15. The leader doesn't think through and act upon what must be done to help a subordinate succeed.
16. The leader fails to set intermediate target dates (milestones) by which to measure progress of subordinates.

17. The leader doesn't introduce new ideas from outside the organization, nor permit or encourage subordinates to do so, thereby freezing the status quo.
18. The leader fails to permit a target of opportunity to be seized in lieu of stated objectives that are less important.
19. The leader is rigid in allowing the knockout of previously agreed-upon goals that have subsequently proven unfeasible, irrelevant, or impossible.
20. The leader doesn't reinforce successful behavior when goals are achieved; the leader doesn't correct unsuccessful behavior when goals are missed.

CHAPTER 9

Organizing

"It almost seems trite to say it, but we must state the obvious. Present problems will not be solved without successful organizations, and organizations cannot be successful without effective leadership."

—Warren Bennis and Burt Nanus[1]

Simply put, organizing is the work we do to put people and tasks together in a structure in hopes of greater achievement by those individuals. All of this is to say that "the probability of a future event occurring increases as effort is applied systematically toward its realization" (Louis A. Allen).

The Ten Commandments of Good Organization

1. Definite and clear-cut assignments should be clearly stated for each position. (Job Descriptions)
2. Assignment should always be coupled with corresponding authority and accountability established. (Delegation)
3. No change should be made in the scope or assignments of a position without a definite understanding to that effect on the part of all persons concerned. (Participation and Communication)
4. No person occupying a single position in the organization should be subject to orders and appraisal from more than one source. (The One-Boss Rule)
5. Orders should never be given to subordinates over the head of a responsible executive. (Follow the System)
6. Criticisms should be made privately. (Courtesy)
7. No dispute or difference between executives or employees as to authority or responsibilities should be considered too trivial for prompt and careful adjudication. (Urgent Action)
8. Changes, disciplinary action and corrections should always be approved and implemented by the executive immediately superior to the one directly responsible. (Developing Managers)
9. No person should ever be required or expected to be at the same time an assistant to and critic of another. (Loyalty)
10. Every person should, whenever practical, be given the assistance and facilities necessary to enable him to maintain an independent check on the quality of his work. (Management Control)

There is a story about a British military team trying to cut down on the manpower used in handling a field cannon. There had always been six men assigned to each cannon, but there were only five jobs. The team studied each job and went to the instruction manuals. From the first edition on, every manual called for a crew of six, even though there seemed to be jobs for only five. Finally they located the man who had written the manual, a retired general, and asked him what the sixth man was supposed to do. He replied, "He holds the horses."

Religious organizations today are perpetuating jobs that exist only because they have existed in the past (back when there were horses)!

Alexander Pope said in 1733, "For forms of government, let fools contest; whatever is best administered is best."

Church Order

> *"To imagine that it is of little importance how the Church should be organized and ordered, then, is manifestly to contradict the apostle. To contend that no organization is prescribed for it is to deny the total validity of the minute directions laid down in these epistles. Nay, this whole point of view is as irrational as it is unbiblical. One might as well say that it makes no difference how a machine is put together — how, for example, a typewriter is disposed in its several parts — because forsooth, the typewriter does not exist for itself, but for the manuscript which is produced by or rather through it. Of course the Church does not exist for itself — that is, for the beauty of its organization, the symmetry of its part, the majesty of its services — it exists for its 'product' and for the 'truth' which has been committed to it and of which it is the support and stay in the world. But, just on that account, not less but more, is it necessary that it be properly organized and equipped and administered, that it may function properly. Beware how you tamper with any machine, lest you mar or destroy its product; beware how you tamper with or are indifferent to the Divine organization and ordering of the Church, lest you thereby mar its efficiency or destroy its power, as the pillar and ground of the truth. Surely you can trust God to know how it is best to organize His Church so that it may perform its functions in the world. And surely you must assert that His ordering of the Church, which is His, is necessary."*
>
> —B. B. Warfield

With the solemn warnings of Pope and Warfield in mind we now turn to the subject of organizing in the work of the church and parachurch ministry.

The traditional hierarchical organizational chart has come under attack in recent years, spearheaded by none other than Robert

Greenleaf. Many successful organizations have abandoned the effort to depict relationships of individuals in a structure in the traditional way in favor of other tools, with particular emphasis on teams.

Once when I was lecturing in London, I had sketched out a traditional organizational chart. One of the participants came up front and took the marker out of my hand and drew an organizational chart in a very nontraditional way. He depicted the leader of the organization on the bottom and then other individuals in the organization above him in an inverted pyramid form. Yet another person in that group suggested that we might show the leader in the middle of a circle, with other leaders fanned out around the central leader.

No matter how you draw the picture, the fact is that effective achievement by groups of human beings requires that each participant know specifically what his tasks are in relationship to others in the structure. In spite of all of the evolution of organizational theory of our day, I do believe that it is too soon to abandon the effort to depict some kind of structure so that people may understand where they fit in the total picture.

Organizational Functional Errors

There are some recurring errors that occur in the attempt to organize. The most glaring error is allowing decisions to drift unnecessarily up the organizational structure, lodging themselves in committees or in the legislative body of the organization. Leaders in healthy organizations are continually pushing decisions downward to the point where the work is actually performed.

Another glaring error is allowing groups to pull decisions and authority to themselves that functionally belong to individuals. If I were a psychologist I might be able to more adequately explain why this phenomenon occurs. I suspect, however, that individuals are loathe to make decisions and prefer the safety of being able to say that the decision was made by a committee or some other group.

Yet another error is failure to recognize the differences in an organizational structure between line and staff. We are forever inserting groups of human beings into the line, increasing the bureaucratic process of organizational life. In a line relationship, individuals are in a superior/subordinate role. On the other hand, the staff relationship indicates "advisory" and "assistant to" by way of role. Not only is it useful to insert groups in the organization into a staff relationship, but it can also be extremely useful for certain individuals. For example, a person who handles the finances of the organization should function in a staff relationship rather than a line relationship.

Often in my consulting I find treasurers and even accountants inserted into the line where they end up making decisions about the work because they hold the purse strings.

Organizational Dynamics

Like job descriptions, organizational structures should be dynamic and never static. A change in the structure can be indicated by a change in objectives; people coming and going or growing or diminishing in their capacity for the work; and even external situations can point to the need for altering the organization's structure.

Another dynamic that is almost universal is the fact that sentiment can actually replace purpose. This is particularly true in religious organizations, even evangelical Christian ones. Sentiment is a powerful force and we are prone to perpetuate a structure because it existed in the past and we have developed a sentimental attachment to it.

The third dynamic at work is the fact that organizations by their very nature and existence seek to perpetuate their existence long after they are needed for the accomplishing of specific purposes.

Centric vs. Radic Organizations

A useful diagnostic tool for an organization's self-examination is the understanding of the differences between centric and radic organizations.

The centric group is one in which the general level of personal concern tends to be greater than the level of group concern. This kind of organization is ingrown and immature.

On the other hand, the radic group is one in which the general level of group concern tends to be greater than the level of personal concern. This is the selfless group, reaching out and beyond itself.

It goes without saying that the Christian organizations should be forever standing guard against the almost universal propensity to deteriorate to a centric group when theoretically we exist as organizations for purposes outside ourselves.

Principles

Principle #1 regarding organization states that the structure always exists for the objectives. The objectives should always exist before the structure and great care should be exercised to ensure that the structure itself is contributing to the accomplishment of the ends for which the organization professes to exist.

Principle #2 is that an individual should be responsible for only the number of people from whom he can effectively receive accountability. This is sometimes referred to in management parlance as, "span of control." How many people one person can oversee in a management role is determined by many factors, not the least of which is the individual's capacity for performing management work. Of course, other factors enter in, such as geography and the type of work being done.

Organizing, putting people and tasks together in a structure, can be a valuable tool in ministry.

CHAPTER 10

Job Descriptions

"People will do a good job if they are provided with management that leads."

—Warren Bennis & Burt Nanus[1]

Three Universal Questions

The three most prevalent questions that Christian workers—or any other workers, for that matter—face are:

"What is my job?"

"How am I doing?"

"Where do I go for help?"

More than any other tool, a job description helps answer these pervasive questions.

Tool, Not Document

Nothing will be more helpful to you and your colleagues with regard to the job description than the simple understanding that this is a tool and not a document. I have often seen organizations wherein job descriptions are a part of the official documents, frequently included as part of by-laws and even in constitutions. The job description should be looked upon as a tool, a way of helping get the job done, and never a document! It should be carried around in a briefcase or kept in a top drawer of a desk, not stored in a vault or bound in leather. It should be dog-eared and well-thumbed, showing signs of use and maybe even have a coffee stain or two. Penciled-in notes, crossed-out sentences and post-it notes are also good signs. A glance at someone's job description probably ought to be a good barometer of how he or she does and views their job, and how they are growing and evolving.

Results of Job Descriptions

Experience teaches us that not only are job descriptions worth the time *and* the paper they are printed on, but they also are an investment in the future. Accurate and realistic job descriptions are absolutely essential to the smooth operation of any organization, secular or religious, volunteers or employees, full or part-time.

The job description is the cornerstone for job definition and scope. A well thought-out, carefully prepared job description will at least accomplish the following:

- spell out duties, responsibilities and limits of authority in a particular position;

- clarify relationships between jobs, thus helping to avoid overlaps and gaps;

- provide the first step toward actual job appraisal;
- help identify future training needs;
- become an invaluable aid in introducing new people to their jobs;
- assist others in the organization in understanding the tasks performed by colleagues as well as themselves;
- serve as a basis for establishing performance standards as they relate to organizational goals;
- be useful in identifying future management development needs;
- serve as a basis for manpower planning, recruiting others for similar positions;
- become a valuable source of information when revision in organizational structure is undertaken;
- serve as a basis for compensation comparison, or some other type of salary rating, within an organization;
- serve as a contract between an employee and his supervisor, showing what each job encompasses and the boundaries of each.

The Big Question

How do you go about getting job descriptions in organizations that have existed for years without them?

First, the chief executive officer of the organization should take the initiative in writing his or her own job description. Since job descriptions are of value as one ascends the organizational structure, it is imperative that we begin at the top. If you are developing an interest in management work prior to that of your pastor or boss, then start where you are and work down. However, remember that it is ideal for the CEO or senior pastor of an organization to write his or her job description first.

Once your job description as CEO has been completed, you will want some kind of approval or ratification. If you have a particularly sharp group of elders, deacons, or board members, you might ask for their ratification, but I do not recommend this. You will probably do better to simply ask for the chairman's approval of what you have done and then proceed with the process.

Who Writes the Description?

Be very careful about this one issue! Never ask a group to write a job description! This is true whether you are dealing with a committee or an entire board. This is one of the places where groups malfunction most seriously. Groups have great difficulty thinking conceptually and the discussion of a job description will degenerate into a mere "duties" list rather than objectives. The order of the words will become more important than the conceptualization of the job.

Once the job description has received some sort of ratification from someone in the organization, perhaps the chairman of the board, then you should make copies for the people reporting directly to you. Take a copy of *your* job description to each one personally, privately, and individually, explaining that you want him or her to know what your job is. Request that the individual follow a similar format in describing on paper what his or her job actually entails. Mind you, this can be done even if a person is deeply entrenched in the job and has been there for 20 years.

Immediately ask the individual whether you might talk with him two weeks hence about his progress in the writing of his own job description. This gets your foot in the door for performance appraisal procedures, and it does so in a most inauspicious and positive manner. Thereafter, you can keep up this periodic dialogue and coaching as well as actual performance evaluation.

Keep in mind that you can only be concerned with job descriptions with the people who report to you. Obviously you hope that your people will take their cue from you and subsequently do similar job description work with their subordinates on their teams. It simply is not possible for you to be responsible for effective job description writing throughout a large organization.

Some of the people who report to you, with whom you have worked in the preparation of job descriptions, will be much more adept than others at following your example with the people below them.

Obviously job descriptions have to be kept up to date. They are not only without value when outdated, but actually become a powerful negative force in the organization's function. The updating can be done in a positive climate by the person in charge, meeting personally and privately with all direct reports.

Abuses to Be Avoided

A serious pitfall to be avoided at all costs is attempting to work with a group of people on job descriptions. It is of utmost importance that this be conducted individually. The tendency will be to get the staff together and to work on the 'project' with several people at once, in the interest of saving time. Don't succumb to this! It will be fatal every time, because it takes away the personalization and removes any opportunity for initiating performance appraisal procedures.

Job descriptions should never be mass-produced. It is utterly pointless for an organization to issue booklets of canned job descriptions. Job descriptions must be tailored to individuals, and as they grow and evolve, the jobs must be altered. This is accomplished by the regularly programmed appraisal review and coaching sessions initiated when the job descriptions are first drawn up by the person doing the work.

A Suggested Format

The following is merely a suggested format to get you started in the job description-writing process. As you evolve and become comfortable with the process, you can alter this format to meet the needs of your organization.

JOB DESCRIPTION

Job title:

Job-holder's name:

Date:

To be update by (date):

JOB PURPOSE
The end result this job exists to accomplish.

DUTIES
Activity, measurable in time and quantity, necessary to accomplish the above.

ORGANIZATIONAL RELATIONSHIPS
Statement of superior and subordinates; i.e., to whom is this position responsible and for what?

QUALIFICATIONS
What a person must be and know to do this job.

TRAINING AND DEVELOPMENT
Reading, training, and experiences planned for this year to better prepare this person to do this job.

    The job title should be as descriptive of the work performed as possible. However, titles are very important to some people and you occasionally may have to accede to an individual's request for a perhaps less descriptive but more impressive-sounding title. That's okay! My concern is much more for performance than protocol.

    Next, the jobholder's name must appear on the job description sheet. A job description is a worthless piece of paper until it is associated with a real, live human being.

    Then, obviously you want to date the job description. But I would urge you to also include a projected obsolescence date by actually writing down the future date by which this job description is to be updated.

    Job Purpose is the most difficult part of the job description. Because we all tend to be much more activities oriented than results oriented, it is difficult for us to state the end results for which this position exists. This particular section of the job description should continue to unfold as long as the individual holds the position. He or she should be vigilant in ongoing efforts to clarify what the end results of the position ought to be.

    Under the heading of Duties, you want to not only list the activities of the job, but along with them list ways to measure them both in time and in quantity. For example, one duty might be to conduct market research, but simply leaving it at that — "conduct market research" — without quantifiers is not enough. Instead, the duty of conducting market research should be followed by an indication of when, how often and perhaps with whom. This part of the job description becomes a checklist, a statement of the employee's personal commitment to achievement and the measurement device one uses to assess and coach the individual in performance appraisal. This is the part of the job description that has the most pencil marks; the most changes. This is the section to which you will later refer to as you sit down with the individual on a weekly or monthly basis to measure and coach and inspire.

Organizational Relationships is the portion of the job description where superior and subordinate relationships are clearly spelled out. The whole idea here is to reinforce your organizational chart, showing to *whom* this person is responsible and *for whom* they are responsible.

The Qualifications part of the job description is a clear statement of what the jobholder must *be* and *know* in order to perform these tasks. In Christian circles, we are tempted simply to list here matters of character and doctrine. This should be avoided. These are "givens" in a Christian organization and will probably be a part of a document somewhere, but should not be included here in this management tool. We are concerned here with the kinds of things that the person is capable of doing or accomplishing.

Finally, the section on Training and Development is a very specific and tailored list of the kinds of reading, training, and experiences planned for a certain period of time for this particular individual, in order to enhance his or her performance. This is highly individualized and personalized and should be continually evolving as the jobholder learns and grows.

Principles

Job descriptions are of value only when they are management tools rather than formal documents.

Job descriptions are of value only to the extent that they are highly personalized and shaped to fit the individual jobholder.

Design the job description to solve specific problems and reach certain performance objectives.

The work of management controlling is the work we do to ensure that performance conforms to plan. Controlling work is often the missing element in management work. It requires time, skills, and tools and is seldom easily attained.

CHAPTER 11

Delegation

"Delegation is the very essence of management work."

—Dick Carlson[1]

An Overview

Snoopy is lying on top of his doghouse. He is lamenting that everybody wants something, everybody complains, and that he has more to do than he can possibly get done. In the final frame of the Schultz comic strip, Snoopy declares, "I hate being head beagle!" Don't we all? If we could spend all of our time preaching, teaching, and counseling we would all be as happy as can be. Those tasks are the chocolate cake of the ministry diet. Unfortunately, a healthy ministry diet also includes lima beans and Brussels sprouts. And that is the work we do to get work done through other people.

One day two of our young sons were ardently trying to identify a strange bird at the feeder on a cold, snowy day. In vain they thumbed through the pages of *Audubon*, looking for a picture resembling what they saw. Suddenly, the bird flew off, leaving two frustrated bird watchers behind.

One of the boys said, "Aw, nuts! Who named all these birds anyway?" The other boy thoughtfully retorted, "God did." The first boy, shaking his head slowly, said, "No He didn't; He told Adam to do it."

That's just like God! And so unlike us. Delegation, in its outworking, is letting someone else do it, and very much resembles God Himself in His relationship with His people.

I was once engaged in an intense conversation with a Japanese pastor. He was frustrated by his relationship with some of my colleagues, Westerners and expatriates. I knew something of the frustration and hoped that by listening I could ameliorate the situation just a bit. In the heat of the discussion, in typical Japanese fashion, he turned to me and said, "There is an old Japanese proverb that goes, 'A wise lord or prince knows even how many ashes are in the kitchen stove.' My friend, is that a good or a bad proverb?" Knowing the importance of our conversation, I hurriedly but silently asked God for wisdom. In retrospect I think He may well have answered and helped me. I replied that in essence that was really an inadequate proverb. I assured him that a wise lord or prince might not know at all how many ashes were in the kitchen stove, but he would certainly know who did know. For the moment I was off the hook!

There are infallible barometers in our lives that indicate when delegation should be pursued diligently and wisely. Any attempt to put a group of people together in the pursuit of mutually agreed upon goals requires delegation. To put it simply, if you are attempting to organize human beings, then delegation becomes an essential ingredient. When you are missing deadlines, you know that it is time to delegate. When you have men and women who need new worlds to conquer in their work, it is time to delegate. When you are performing trivial tasks that others could do if trained and allowed to do so, it is time to delegate. When you are overworked, it is time to delegate. And finally, when crises become frequent, it is time to delegate.

Not All of Your Problems Are Spiritual

Did you know that not all of your problems are spiritual in nature? That is to say, that prayer and other spiritual exercises will not provide the solution to all of your ministry problems. Indeed, the problems that confront most of us most seriously relate to the inevitable task that we must eventually face: getting work done through other people.

One of the most valuable discoveries any Christian leader can make is that management is the set of skills and tools that can be acquired and developed regardless of one's spiritual gifts. Management work is indicated by position, not by spiritual gifts or natural proclivity. If you have accepted the position of pastor, president, or executive director, then it is incumbent upon you, by virtue of that position, to learn how to plan, lead, organize, and control.

Consider now this one aspect of the management process: delegation. The reason more people don't delegate is because of something that goes on *inside* of them rather than what goes on *around* them. A common explanation given for the failure to delegate is that there are not competent people within the organization who can take on pieces of your work. To put it another way, our failure to delegate is almost always emotional rather than logistical.

The Scriptures have many illustrations of competent delegation. Consider Joseph, Nehemiah, the apostles in Acts, the teachings of the apostle Paul with regard to passing the word and the work on to other men, and the example of our Lord Jesus Christ Himself.

It is usually sheer desperation that drives most of us to the point of being willing to pay the price emotionally to do the work of delegating. It is at that point that knowledge becomes critical. We must understand how delegation works. What are the essential ingredients? What are the pitfalls to be avoided?

The Three Essentials of Delegation

Delegation consists of three essential elements:

- first, the *assignment* of the task;
- second, the *authority* commensurate with the responsibility; and
- third, establishing clear lines of *accountability*.

The *assignment* is the process whereby another human being takes on a part of your tasks willingly and commits himself to assist you in the accomplishment of a larger task. It is at this point in the process that a job description becomes valuable. A clear understanding of the tasks is essential and very often missed, resulting in confusion and frustration on the part of both parties.

Authority is an essential ingredient because it gives its holder the right or power to perform the task in question. If you get someone to agree to the performance of a task but you do not specify his scope or power, then you merely encumber your own life because that person will keep coming back to you for decisions.

It is at the third point of delegation that most of us create the most havoc: we omit the *accountability* process. It is the sole responsibility of the leader doing the delegating to ensure that clear lines of accountability are established. Failure to do so results in abandonment of the task and the person who has agreed to perform the work. It is at this point that most efforts at delegation fail. This aspect of delegation, like most all management work, must be done one-on one. Only in private are we able to do the delicate work of coaching and correcting.

Barriers to Delegation

Very often we miss the all-important management task of delegation because we are all members of the body of Christ. We are members one of another, we are brothers and sisters, we are all priests before God. This can cause us to forget the fact that God has ordained that some should lead and others should follow and that each should fulfill his role in compliance with God's gifts to him and her. Delegation does not violate our relationships, it enhances them.

The Authority to Delegate

Once we have overcome the barriers to delegation, the question becomes, by what authority do we delegate?

First there is the authority derived from *position*. If you have a title or a position don't belittle your position, don't deprecate it; rather, for the glory of God and the furtherance of the gospel, take advantage of it.

The second source of authority for delegation is *character*. This is your personal credit rating with your team.

The third source of authority is your *personality*. This is the you seen by the other person. The more pleasant, the easier you are to live with, the more apt people are to do the work you request of them.

The fourth source of authority is *your own competence*. Be careful on this one. The competency at issue here is your competency as a leader, the work you do on behalf of your followership. You need not necessarily be competent in the work that you are asking the other person to perform; that is far from necessary. But you must be very competent in the work of managing and leading.

How to Delegate

Joe Batten, noted management consultant, once said in my presence that the way to delegate effectively was to:

- get acceptance on the part of the other person and ensure reciprocal understanding;
- state the end result desired in the task and not the activities themselves;
- put the individual on his own and let him perform and even fail if necessary; and
- follow through.

Very good advice.

Principles

A person should delegate only to the extent that he can effectively receive accountability and effectively coach toward end results. This is called "span of control."

Authority should always equal responsibility in the delegation process. If you don't pass authority on to the individual adequate to perform the work, then you merely encumber your own life because the person will be coming back to you repeatedly for permission to act.

The person delegating should always assume responsibility for the performance of the individual to whom the task has been delegated.

This ensures that the person delegating will not abandon the individual and will do the coaching and training necessary to ensure success.

Each person should have only one person to whom he answers with regard to the performance of that task. This is sometimes referred to as the principle of single reporting relationships.

Finally, the person delegating is solely responsible to elicit accountability from the person to whom the task has been given. This is true even though he or she is a volunteer. The person doing the delegating bears the brunt of eliciting accountability in a way that will cause the individual to grow and derive satisfaction from the performance of the task.

Joseph G. Mason once said the keys to successful delegation are three: know what and how much to delegate, delegate in depth, and communicate effectively.

We cannot get inside another person, but we can create powerful influences. When we create powerful influences within a system that is beneficial to all concerned, we can expect results that will be gratifying to all involved.

Effective management work probably has never come naturally to anyone. It is a set of skills and tools that require discipline, study, effort, and consistency. Maybe Snoopy understood all of this, and that's why he hated being head beagle!

Managing Volunteers

By far the greatest untapped resource for ministry today has got to be that huge reservoir of volunteers that we have yet to recruit, train, motivate and integrate into our ministries. The problem for most of us is that we often conclude that it is easier to do it ourselves than to recruit volunteers to share in the load. To reason this way is to be short-sighted, to say the least.

Involving volunteers in our work is a complicated process, but if we learn how to do it, it can provide returns out of proportion to the original effort and cost involved.

There are four steps that are absolutely essential in the utilization of volunteers: recruitment, assignment, authority, and accountability.

Recruitment — By far the most important step in this process is the recruiting of volunteers in the right way. It will help if we distinguish clearly between volunteers who are going to take on the leadership of some aspect of ministry and volunteers who are going to do hands-on work that requires no leadership of others.

It might help if we draw a line between managing and supervising. Someone has said that to manage is to plan, lead, organize, and control. On the other hand, to supervise is to direct closely and personally. If we need people to move tables and chairs from one location to another, then all we provide is supervision. However, if we ask someone to take charge of a ministry and involve others along the way, then the type of guidance we provide is that of management.

Recruiting must be done the right way, bearing in mind the distinctions cited above. It is perfectly acceptable to recruit people who will be supervised just by making an appeal from the podium or in a publication. If you are going to recruit people for leadership roles, then it must be done one-on-one. It is unrealistic to expect that we are going to recruit truly competent people with mass appeals. We should clearly understand the work that needs to be done and then identify the people who come to mind who might be prospects. Once that has been done, those people should be approached privately and personally, never by mass appeal.

The next step in successful recruiting has to do with who is going to approach the potential volunteer. The rule is that the person who is going to be providing the oversight of the volunteer should always be the one to make the contact and request for volunteer assistance. This establishes the right relationship from the start.

Assignment — Now that you have identified a potential volunteer and have received their agreement to work with you, you will want to communicate clearly what their assignment is. This is the process wherein another human being takes on a part of your tasks willingly and commits to assisting you in the accomplishment of a larger task. A job description becomes very helpful at this point. A clearly spelled-out description of the volunteer's task(s) will avert later misunderstandings, confusion and frustration on the part of both parties.

Authority — This is an essential ingredient in the managing of volunteers. Authority confers upon the volunteer the right or power to perform the task(s) in question. If you persuade someone to volunteer to perform a job, but you never get around to specifying that volunteer's scope or power, you have merely encumbered your own life, because that volunteer is going to keep coming back to you for permission to act.

Accountability — Here is where most of us create the most havoc in the managing of volunteers: we omit the accountability process. It is the sole responsibility of the leader who is doing the recruiting and subsequently the delegating of responsibility to ensure that clear lines of accountability are established. Failure of the leader to create and maintain lines of accountability is equal to abandoning the task and the volunteer who has agreed to perform the task. It is at this point that most efforts at delegation fail.

Here is why I think we quite often miss the all-important management task of delegating responsibility. We allow for the fact that in the local church we are all members of the body — we are all members of one another; we are all brothers and sisters; we are all priests before God — to cause us to forget that God has ordained that some should lead and others should follow.

Once we have overcome the barriers to delegation, the question becomes, By what authority do we delegate? The following, by the way, applies to delegation in all settings: volunteers and staff.

There are four sources of authority to support a leader's delegating. The first is the authority derived from position. If you have a title or a position, do not belittle or deprecate it. Rather, for the glory of God and the furtherance of the gospel, take advantage of it.

The second source of authority for delegation is character. This is your personal credit rating with your team.

The third source of authority is your personality. This is the 'you' seen by the other person—your volunteer. The more pleasant you are, the easier to live with, the more likely are volunteers to be willing to do the work you request of them.

The fourth source of authority to delegate is your own competence. Be careful on this one. The competency at issue here is your competence as a leader — the work you do on behalf of those you lead. You need not necessarily be competent in the work that you are asking your volunteer to perform. That is far from necessary. But you must be very competent in the work of managing and leading.

Key Principles for Managing Volunteers

1. A leader recruiting a volunteer should delegate to the individual only to the extent that he can effectively receive accountability and effectively coach toward end results.

2. Authority should always equal responsibility in the delegation process. If you don't pass on authority to your volunteer that is adequate to allow them to perform the job, you wind up with a volunteer who is constantly hobbled by the need to ask you for permission to do this or that.

3. The person delegating should always assume responsibility for the performance of the volunteer to whom the task has been delegated. This ensures that the leader delegating will keep in steady contact with the volunteer, doing the coaching and training necessary to ensure success.

4. Your volunteer should have one designated person to whom he looks for guidance and answers with regard to the performance of the task. This is sometimes referred to as the principle of single reporting relationships.

5. The leader who is delegating is solely responsible to elicit accountability from the volunteer to whom the task has been given, remembering that work relationships with volunteers need to be handled with a great deal of sensitivity. The leader must learn to elicit accountability in a way that will cause the volunteer to grow and derive satisfaction from the performance of the task.

CHAPTER 12

Development

"Where there is no vision, the people perish. Where there is no plan, the vision perishes. Where there is no money the plan perishes."

The lack of money for ministry is a pervasive problem for Christian ministries. There is probably no more acutely felt need in Christian organizations than the need for money.

You probably have been a part of a scene similar to the following. A group of men and women sit around a table. It may be a staff meeting or committee meeting. The subject is funding for the organization. The need for money is urgent. Individuals are encouraged to suggest ideas as to how money might be procured. One person suggests this, another person suggests that, and the group frantically looks for something, some activity or event, that will quickly produce funds for the emergency at hand. Almost always the quest is for large sums of money that can be obtained rapidly from a very few people.

The truth is, there is no quick fix with regard to money for ministry. I remember talking to the head of a ministry in Pennsylvania one day. He had told me that he was in dire straits and needed money if his work was to continue. I explained that our organization had devised a six-month training program whereby we would meet with his organization one day per month for six months and in between the training sessions we would talk on the telephone, providing coaching, so as to get the organization up and running financially. He replied with vehemence, urgency in his voice, that six months was out of the question. He said he had to have money by next Friday to make payroll! He turned down my invitation to embark on a six-month development training program. I learned a few months later that the organization had closed its doors. In an atmosphere of panic, leaders of organizations almost always make the wrong choices about fund development and sacrifice the future on the altar of the immediate.

The Right Attitude Toward Development

The beginning point of healthy, successful development is having the right attitude in two categories. First, there must be a heartfelt belief in the value of the organization. It is highly unlikely that anyone is going to raise large sums of money on behalf of an endeavor in which he or she does not believe and whose integrity and importance he does not himself embrace.

The second attitude accepts the fact that there is absolutely no shortage of money. We lament that there are too many organizations in our community attempting to raise money. Unemployment might be high. All of these scandals in charities across the nation have made it harder for us to raise money. The cost of living has soared, and people don't have money to give. The excuses and rationalizations multiply. The fact is, there is no shortage of money. In fact, there exists all of the money that is needed for ministries of value.

Many of us who are leaders in Christian organizations have never had much money and probably never will. Most of us have lived on modest salaries and have had to be careful in the use of our money just to get by and to care for our families. We take our own economic situation and unconsciously impose its limitations upon people around us. Until we come to grips with the fact that there are plenty of people with plenty to give and the willingness to do so as well, we will never be successful in fundraising.

The Three Tasks of Development

A Presbyterian pastor in St. Louis who is very knowledgeable concerning development says that there are only three tasks in development: *win, keep* and *lift*.

Winning the donor is conspicuously the beginning point in development. This is the complicated and delicate work of first finding new people who have never given to the organization, and informing them of the good we seek to bring about, with the result that they give for the first time. It is probably very obvious to you that this is the most difficult, costly, and labor-intensive aspect of development.

Some have said that it costs a great deal more to acquire a donor than to keep and lift an existing donor. A wise development strategy is to monitor carefully how many new, first-time contributors have come on board.

The second task is that of *keeping* the donor. We lose donors by what we call "donor abuse." There are a thousand ways, I suppose, to abuse donors. Mind you, there are many people who will continue to give to your organization no matter how poorly you treat them. However, it cannot possibly be pleasing to God for us to abuse donors through our ignorance or slothfulness. Some of the most common abuses include the failure to get thank-you letters and receipts to donors within 48 hours of receiving the gift; misspelling their names; using impersonal "Dear Friend" type letters; and the list goes on and on. Good development work is extremely conscientious when it comes to nurturing and retaining existing donors.

The third task of development is to *lift* the donor. Strategic development work assumes that if someone sends the organization a check for $25.00, that he would like to give more. If they are able to do so, if you treat them properly, and if you ask them to, they will give again. Obviously, if you learn that they are unable to give more, you certainly should never press them to do so. Consider every gift as a test. The donor is testing your organization: "How will they treat me as a result of my gift? What kind of information will they provide me now that I have given? How professionally competent is this organization?" Assume that every donor is asking these kinds of questions about your organization.

Friends, Not Just Funds

It is a truism that development is the work of cultivating and nurturing friendships, not just the procurement of funds. This must undergird everything we do in development. It is essential that we apply all of the principles of relationship building in the process of gathering funds.

Development Work Is Ministry!

I spent the first ten years of my career as a pastor. When I announced that I was departing to go to Far Eastern Gospel Crusade, now SEND International, an elderly lady in my church told me that she was sorry to see me leave the ministry, but she wished me well. I'm sure the dear lady meant well. But her words reflect a serious deficiency in our understanding of the many facets of work necessary for ministry to be accomplished.

The simple truth is that this whole matter of Christians giving so that ministry might occur is the grand design of God Himself. This is not simply a clever device of man. It is God's own plan. When we come to understand this we are then prepared to embrace development as ministry. We do not then see development as opposed to preaching, teaching, counseling, and the other things from which we derive so much satisfaction.

I once encouraged a staff member of a para-church ministry to assist in donor cultivation and donor relationships. This man was very competent in preaching and teaching the word of God. When I suggested that he might help with donor relations, he said that he would rather be assigned the task of taking out the garbage every day! Another ministry leader said to me one day that he was very proud of the fact that he had never once asked anybody for money! And yet, both of the organizations represented by these men were in serious financial difficulties.

The Bible is replete with instances of God's servants asking for funds for God's work. It seems to me that it is absolutely essential for us to come to a heartfelt acceptance of the fact that development is ministry just as much as preaching, teaching, and counseling.

My friend Dave Coleman, regional director of the Pacific Northwest Youth for Christ, speaks with clarity on the subject of development: "A Youth For Christ (YFC) donor is a person whose concerns and values match those that are addressed by our YFC mission and ministry and who makes a financial investment in YFC so that together we can see it happen. Donors are truly our important partners in accomplishing the mission of YFC. Development is the ongoing ministry of discovering, informing, inspiring, challenging, building and maintaining relationships with those people in order that both their objectives and ours are met."

Development Defined

Aristotle said that all of our difficulties come from our failure to define terms. He may have been right. I have struggled for years to adequately define *development.* The definition I offer here is subject to revision and, I hope, improvement in the days to come.

Simply put, development is consistently doing the right things, in the right sequence, and in the right proportions, resulting in adequate funding for ministry while bringing great glory to God and great satisfaction to the people who give money.

Now, allow me to break this down and discuss each vital component.

The first key word is *consistently.* Nowhere does the law of the farm apply more meaningfully than to development work. What you sow, you will reap! You must prepare the soil, plant the seed, fertilize and nurture the plant, if you expect to reap a harvest. We must be consistent day in and day out, through good times and bad times, and at all times of the year. Consistency is absolutely vital!

Yet all of us have sat in meetings where we were discussing how to cut expenditures so as to avoid going deeper into the red. Inevitably the first thing to go is the development department.

The second part of the definition is *doing the right things.* The question then becomes, "How do we know what the right things are?" There are only two ways to find out. One way is to experiment ourselves and ferret out the failures and discover what works. Needless to say, this is very expensive and time consuming. The other way is to learn from the experience of others. The work of philanthropy has been going on for thousands of years and for many, many years innumerable successful individuals have put their discoveries into print. Nearly everything we need to know about what works and what does not work in development someone has put into a book or an article. Yet I have met countless development people who have never read Seymour, Greenfield, Panas, Lord, Rosso, or any of the other dozens of highly experienced and knowledgeable authors. Many development pratitioners that I have met do not subscribe to *The Chronicle of Philanthropy, Fund Raising Management, Non-Profit Times, Non-Profit Alert,* or any of the other dozens of periodicals that provide helpful information about what the right things are.

The next part of the definition refers to doing things *in the right sequence.* Many times when I am invited into an organization to consult, the organization is desperate for large sums of money quickly. Usually they start out by saying that they want to immediately begin soliciting foundations or acquiring large gifts from major donors. Often organizations say that they want to launch a capital campaign to raise large sums of money for expansion. More often than not, these organizations have failed to realize that it is not possible to conduct a capital campaign when there is not an adequate donor base in place. You cannot launch a planned giving program when you do not have donors who have been with you over time and who have not yet given significant amounts of money. The right sequence is positively indispensable. You have to start with a case statement, progress to building and maintaining a segmented mailing list, cultivating entry-level donors, nurturing donors to keep them and eventually lift them, and then move on to the cultivating of multi-year sustained donors. Only then are you prepared to move into capital campaigns and planned and deferred giving. Sequence is all important!

The next part of the definition of development refers to doing things *in the right proportions.* An organization can easily fall into the trap of spending a disproportionate amount of money on direct mail or on the promotion of planned giving instruments or foundation solicitation.

When visiting with the principals of a prospective client organization, I learned they were considering using me to help them perform foundation solicitation because they needed large sums of money and they needed it quickly. They, like many other organizations, failed to realize that far and away the great bulk of charitable giving comes from individuals. A comparatively small amount comes from foundations and corporations. They had their proportions wrong.

The next part of the definition refers to *bringing great glory to God.* Good development work is committed from the outset to doing everything under the blazing scrutiny of the Holy Spirit. We are committed to doing and saying absolutely nothing that would in the slightest grieve the Holy Spirit. This commitment answers all of the questions relating to the law and ethics.

The final part of the definition pertains to bringing *great satisfaction to the people who give money*. Our donors are our partners, indeed equal partners, along with everyone else in the organization. We treat them that way. We spell their names correctly. We send them a receipt immediately when we receive their gift. We answer any question they might ask about our work. We gladly give to friend and foe alike copies of our audited financials. We tell them what the executives' salaries are, if they ask. We have no secrets. We thank them in meaningful ways and treat them as equal partners.

The Six Components of Development

Theology — Every organization should have its own theology of development. Theology of development may or may not be written down but should be clearly understood by the participants in development work. These are the absolutes with regard to fund raising, derived from the Scriptures, and cannot be violated.

Philosophy — Our philosophy of development will reflect our understanding of matters relating to ethics and prudence. These are matters that are binding upon us in development work but they could conceivably, under certain circumstances, be changed.

Strategy — This is a statement of what we are going to do and in what sequence and with what priority we will approach the work of development.

Systems — This refers to all of the procedures necessary to accomplish development work. In this day and age, it inevitably involves the computer. But there are many other systems: how the mail is opened; how checks get to the bank; how the mail gets out the front door and to the post office.

Services — The larger the organization, the more intricate is the integration of all of the services that impinge upon the development function. This will involve such activities as computer services, accounting procedures, publications, and public relations activities.

Controls — This concerns the work that is done to ensure that performance conforms to plan, and that activities are well within the boundary of the theology and the philosophy of development.

Why People Give

I cannot possibly overemphasize the fact that people give to vision! As leaders of Christian organizations we are sometimes overburdened with the needs we face within our organization. Therefore, we tend to present our needs to donors. Donors are not inspired by needs. They are inspired by vision.

There is a story in development circles of one of America's most prominent Christian leaders who had presented to a friend his vision for an enormous undertaking that his organization was contemplating. It is reported that after the presentation the man wrote out a check for one million dollars. In the "memo" section of the check, he penned, "For Dr. So & So's vision." That's it! People give to vision, not needs.

There are other dynamics at work that cause people to give. People give money based upon:

- their value system,

- their awareness level, and

- their priority list.

Their value system — Each of us has our own system of values that determines where we give our money. A dear friend of mine who gives away large sums of money each year values personal, one-on-one evangelism very highly. He is not inclined to give toward buildings or endowments. He wants his money to go to support individuals who are presenting Christ to unbelievers. Another man I know was in World War II, fighting the Japanese. After the war, he became a Christian and has devoted his life and his money to evangelism and church planting in Japan. Good development work recognizes people's individual value systems and accommodates their preferences in every way possible. Our task is to sift through people until we find those who share the values of our work.

Their awareness level — It is essential that we make prospective donors who share our value system aware of who we are and what we are doing. With regard to existing donors, we must keep our organization ever before them in every way possible. The use of mail is probably the best vehicle at our disposal to keep our work and its name in front of our constituency. One of my clients is using E-mail to thank donors for gifts and to provide information that would otherwise not be possible.

A word needs to be inserted here concerning organization newsletters. Recently I was reviewing the materials of a prospective client and discovered that his donor newsletter was also a house organ, an event promotion sheet and an inspiration tool actually involving sermonettes. Big mistake!

A newsletter should be aimed at prospective donors and donors only. Don't try to make a newsletter an in-house instrument, a vehicle for promoting upcoming events, and a request for contributions. Every single, solitary word in a newsletter should be directed only at prospective donors and existing donors. The contents of a newsletter should be only information and inspiration. As you contemplate the copy for your next newsletter, try to imagine that someone who has never heard of your organization is picking up your publication for the first time. You want to convey to them as quickly as possible the following three things:

- what exactly the good is that your organization is bringing about;
- which people within the organization are making it happen;
- which people are governing and endorsing the organization's work.

Your newsletter should identify the officers of the organization, your board of trustees or directors, and your council of reference.

Members of your council of reference are high-visibility Christian leaders who, by use of their name on your publication, will lend immediate credibility to your organization.

Remember that your newsletter must be designed to increase the awareness of both existing and future donors of your organization. Therefore, you are much better off sending out 12 monthly newsletters per year (8 1/2" x 11", printed on both sides), than to send only two newsletters a year that stretch to eight pages in length. Your goal is to increase donors' awareness of your work.

Their priority list — Assuming that you have found an individual who shares the values of your ministry and you have successfully made him aware of you, then your next task is to ascend his priority list. Most prospective donors to your work are already giving money to their local church and to other ministries. You rise on their priority list by the image your project—via your newsletter, among other things—and the way you treat them.

To Ask or Not to Ask

When I began my ministry in missions in the 1950s, the influence of George Mueller was still very strong in the evangelical circles in which I moved. George Mueller, you may remember, was the gentleman in England who provided care for so many orphans and did so by asserting that he never asked for money and that God provided the funds without his having to ask. Mueller indeed may never have asked for money, but he was a prolific writer and distributor of leaflets and books. In his repeated giving of testimony in his writings of how God provided funds without him having to ask, he was in effect asking by telling people that he never asked. My friend, George Verwer, founder of Operation Mobilization, said of George Mueller, "Perhaps he never asked for money, but he was a lightning rod of communications!"

In my early days of ministry in missions, the development experts leaned toward a policy of not asking and instead simply provided what was called "information without solicitation." The debate was endless as to what constituted solicitation. At what point do you cross the line from merely giving information about needs to asking for people to give to meet those needs?

Now, at the turn of the century, I notice in a recent publication of the Interdenominational Foreign Missions Association that the position is "information without *strong* solicitation." So, there has been in my long career an evolution with regard to the asking for funds for the furtherance of the gospel.

It seems to me that at the heart of the question before us has to be what will please the Lord and what might grieve the Lord. There are so many examples in both the Old Testament and the New Testament of God's servants asking for funds from God's people to further God's work. The issues, it seems to me, include what might grieve the Lord, what might taint the reputation of the organization doing the asking, and what might offend the intelligence and sensitivities of the person being asked. It seems to me that the issue is much more philosophical than theological in nature. If I could convey any single message to ministry leaders today it would be that it's OK to ask!

Integrated Financial Development System (IFDS)

My colleague in Leadership Resource Group, Jim Holdman, first introduced me to his Integrated Financial Development System many years ago. It is a variation on the James Greenfield model published in his classic work. Few bits of development information have been more beneficial to me than Holdman's IFDS model. In one glance at his pyramid, one can visualize not only the totality of development work, but also the sequence in which it must be implemented.

```
                    /\
                   /  \
                  /    \
                 / Planned & \
                / Deferred Gift \
               /   Programs      \
              /  Capital Campaign  \
             /  Investment Programs  \
            / Multi-Year Sustained Program \
           /    Current Gift Program        \
          /  Master Communications Schedule   \
         /     Segmented Mailing Lists          \
        /         Case Statement                  \
       /        Development Audit                   \
      /_____\
```

The Case Statement

The case statement is the basic document which sets forth in marketing terms a summary of the organization, the needs it fills, the cost, and the urgency for support. In short, it is the organization's sales manual.

A good case statement should be a handy reference guide for the writing of all brochures and media presentations. Its contents become the editorial source from which all communications to the public are patterned.

The present and prospective constituency is constantly bombarded with information. Only those organizations or institutions that tell their story well, tell it simply, and tell it often will penetrate the informational overload and motivate the constituency to a response.

Every organization has a program to disseminate information, whether planned or unplanned. The question is not whether an organization has one, but whether the information given out is good or poor. Poor information, like good information, generates opinions. An organization must give out good information in a uniform manner to create confidence and credibility with its constituents.

The case statement helps the organization's professionals and volunteers know factually who they are and the direction in which they are moving. Simply stated, it answers the questions before they are asked. Every organization or institution needs an overall case statement, plus additional individual case statements for each separate project.

A good case statement will answer at least the following questions:

1. What brought the organization or institution to where it is today?

2. What needs does the organization meet?

3. What is the organization's mission?

4. What is the future of the organization?

5. How much does it cost to meet the organization's objectives?

6. How is the organization supported?

A good case statement is never considered to be in its final form. There will continue to be ways in which the case statement can be improved upon to better communicate the organization's message.

I'm often asked how long a case statement should be. The answer is very simply that it should be as long as is necessary to communicate the data you wish to proffer to a targeted audience. Your complete case statement might take six pages or it might require thirty pages. The issue is content and the adequacy of telling the story rather than length.

There will be some instances where you will want to give the entire case statement to a donor or prospective board member. In other instances, you will merely excerpt pertinent sections, depending upon your readership.

Over the years, I have critiqued countless case statements from my clients. Far and away, the most common case statement deficiency has been the absence of passion. I remember hearing one of my clients make a presentation of his ministry to a small audience. I would be hard-pressed to remember a more impassioned statement of the good for which an organization existed to accomplish. I was deeply moved. Yet, when I critiqued his case statement, I found it to be almost totally devoid of fire. He was much better at speaking about his work than he was at writing about it. Build passion and urgency into your written case statement!

Allow me to offer in summary form a few writing tips for preparing your case statement.

1. Write factually, but with emotion.
2. Be complete, yet brief.
3. Write with a sense of urgency.
4. Be convincing.
5. Answer the most frequently asked questions about your organization.
6. Use good grammar, but ensure a conversational, personal tone.
7. Use a flowing style, weaving in human-interest material.
8. Use pictures and charts.
9. Develop the case statement story a topic at a time.
10. Be positive.
11. Do not criticize the competition, but point out the value of your work.
12. Show how the reader of your case statement can help the organization achieve its objectives.

The Segmented, Managed Mailing List

The mailing list is the heart and lungs of the development anatomy. It is impossible to have a healthy development program without a growing, segmented and well-managed mailing list.

Yet, few aspects of development are more misunderstood and abused than the mailing list. I was once asked to conduct a development audit for a sizable ministry that had a mailing list of almost 50,000 names. Everybody on the list got everything the organization published. The process not only wasted an enormous amount of money each year on people who were not even remotely interested in the organization, but it also insulted people who made significant gifts of money who should have received special, personalized communiqués. When I suggested to the CEO that he should segment his mailing list and send only targeted mailings, his response was that he wanted everybody to get everything because he had no way of knowing what their interest might be. This CEO was one of the most frugal and dedicated servants of Christ I have ever known. Yet, he was willing to waste many thousands of dollars every year by his refusal to segment his list.

When we adequately manage a segmented mailing list, we are not only being prudent in our expenditures, we are also acquiescing to the preferences of our donors and prospective donors. At issue is not only frugality, but also donor sensitivity.

When I began my work in para-church ministry, list segmentation was almost unheard of. The device we used to address mail was a clumsy invention called the Addressograph. Heavy metal plates would drop down through a chute, falling onto a carbon ribbon, making an inked impression on the envelope or newsletter. Some of my younger readers will have only a comic idea what this contraption looked like or how it worked. In its day, it was considered a timesaving step up from hand addressing. What a different era that was!

Today, a vital part of achieving high-touch in our development activities is becoming high-tech. As technology has evolved it has become possible for us to highly personalize our mailings and thereby save money. We can now fire a target-finding rifle rather than an erratic shotgun.

Several years ago, Leadership Resource Group commissioned Synergy Development Systems, Inc., of Royal Palm Beach, Florida, to create development software that specifically incorporates the tracker system of the IFDS mailing list model. This model enables an organization to acquire a great number of names of "suspects" at varying times of the month or year, and integrate them into a process wherein they are informed of the work and moved to the track where they are then solicited. If they give, they are reckoned to be partners in the ministry; if they do not give after a series of specific solicitations, their names are moved to the "dead file."

One thing is sure: you are going to lose donors. They are going to die, move away, or have their interest diverted; they might even get mad at you and stop giving! A healthy development philosophy asks every day how many new names have been added to the mailing list.

The first step is to ensure that all of the friends of your organization are continually on the alert for new names that can be given to the organization to be processed through the "intro" track and subsequently the solicitation track. Your sources from which to draw new names include your board, former board members, staff, referrals, events that your group stages, and even purchased lists. The IFDS/Synergy Development Systems software allows you to have a steady flow of new names all the time, yet those names can be at varying stages of progression through the tracks. Names are put into the intro track where they then receive very specialized and individualized treatment (analysis) before they are moved on to the solicitation track.

Let's imagine an ideal scenario. Say the name of Mr. Smith has been brought to you. Mr. Smith should first receive a best foot forward-type letter with your very best brochure, saying that you have reason to believe that Mr. Smith might want to know more about your organization and the good it brings about. This first 'intro' track letter has no solicitation. Then, in about a month, Mr. Smith should receive a copy of your newsletter. Remember that your newsletter is designed exclusively for donors and prospective donors. Content of the newsletter is limited to information and inspiration, and always carries a bridge-building or "credibility column." This column specifically includes the names of your board members, key staff—especially senior staff—and a list of your council of reference. After another month goes by, Mr. Smith will get a second carefully crafted personal letter from the CEO of your organization. When 30 more days have gone by, Mr. Smith will be the recipient of your next newsletter, and so on. You may mail four or five or six pieces to Mr. Smith before he is automatically moved to the next track: solicitation.

Once Mr. Smith has been properly "prepped" by having received a predetermined array of well-timed mailings and his name has been placed in the solicitation track, he may be asked twice or even three times (depending on how your organization has programmed the system) to give. If Mr. Smith does give, then he is automatically moved to the "contributor" track. In this track, Mr. Smith receives his receipt promptly along with a kid-glove-treatment letter of thanks. After all, Mr. Smith has become your partner, indeed, your equal partner in the ministry. If after two or three solicitations Mr. Smith does not give, then he is automatically put into the "dead file." Of course, you never throw a name away. You keep these non-donors who have passed through the intro track, and then later, when you are flush with development funds, you can revisit your dead file and experiment with mailing to every fifth name or so to check again to see if Mr. Smith's interest can be kindled.

Keep in mind that there will be occasions when people become donors through whatever means, but have not gone through your intro track. Great care should be exercised to ensure that your software notifies you of anyone who has not given previously. In other words, *any first-time gift to your organization should not only be receipted promptly, but with very special attention.* A first-time donor should get a special letter over the signature of the CEO, welcoming him as a partner in the work. This is called a "welcome packet." It should not be considered extravagant for an organization to spend ten or even fifteen dollars on a welcome packet.

Once Mr. Smith has moved to the contributor track, there are several important factors to be considered. Perhaps the most commonly abused aspect of donor relations is the failure to send a receipt immediately. Some of my clients have progressed to the point that they can turn receipts around the same day the gift comes in. That makes a good impression on donors. Directly, it says to the donor that your organization is efficient and competent; indirectly it suggests that your organization will use the gift wisely. It makes the donor feel important, too, to be responded to so quickly.

I remember working with a client in Indiana many years ago. When I first conducted my development audit for these folks, I discovered that they were sending receipts out only twice a year. I was appalled and dumbfounded. In short order, I convinced this group to begin daily receipting. To their very great surprise, many donors who had been giving monthly were now giving two gifts a month. One of the men, upon learning this fact, asked whether someone should call these donors and tell them that they were giving twice a month. My counsel to them was that their donors knew how many gifts they were giving! After all, it was their money.

This kind of problem very often is the result of having the receipting process in the control of the business office. Receipting is a development function. Whenever possible, I suggest that my clients move the sending out of receipts into the hands of the development office ASAP. People who work in the business office are compliance-oriented, not development-oriented. Mind you, we need compliance-oriented professionals to handle accounting-type functions. But they should not be the ones to also devise development strategies and tactics. A friend of mine jokingly referred to the folks in the numbers business as "bean counters." But he called those in development "bean growers."

Another important element of the IFDS mailing philosophy has to do with lapsed donor intervention. It is imperative that your development reports tell you on a daily basis when donors' giving patterns are interrupted. When there is an interruption, some intervention must occur. Your source codes will tell you who might be the right person to do the intervening. It may be a staffer whose personal support has been disrupted and in that case, he or she is the obvious party to take action. Certainly, for the very largest donors, it might be that the CEO should make contact. In most instances it will be the chief development officer who will act.

The key to lapsed donor intervention is quick response. Let's say our Mr. Smith has been giving steadily on a monthly basis, but suddenly stops giving for two or three months. A letter from you should be sent explaining that Mr. Smith is more important than the money he gives and that your reason for writing is simply to inquire about the change. Has Mr. Smith become ill? Did he lose his job? Is Mr. Smith mad at you? Of course, the best intervention is face-to-face, but that's not always possible. Sometimes, a telephone call is useful.

Eight years ago, I sat down at my desk to write checks for the month. I had decided not to send checks to five organizations that I had been giving to for quite some time. One of the organizations had been receiving checks from me almost monthly for nearly 15 years. I had been a donor to another organization for only a few months. I decided that I would wait and see what these five organizations did in response to the cessation of my giving. Now, eight years later, not one of the five organizations has called me or written to me or made contact of any sort. That is donor abuse at its very worst. Oh yes, I am still on the mailing lists of all five organizations! Think of the money they have wasted on me over the years.

Another important element of the IFDS mailing strategy is what we call the 'insulated' track. The Synergy Development System software makes this insulated track very easy and powerful to use. Every organization wants its newsletters to go to the families of staff members, prayer partners, personal friends, and the fraternal list. These people may or may not be on the contributor track. They may or may not have been asked to give. The point is that you want to isolate the people to whom you write concerning promotion of events, prayer requests, and the like. You need some kind of insulation of these names in order to do that.

A further word needs to be said concerning the management of the contributor track. I cannot possibly overemphasize how important it is that you turn receipts around quickly. The ideal is to respond to every gift the same day you receive it. Most organizations can do this with technology being what it is today. Certainly no organization should ever let the return of receipts extend beyond 48 hours.

Receipts with thank-you letters should be among the best-looking pieces that your organization produces. The money that your donors give is the lifeblood of your organization. Every consideration should be given to making the giving process as convenient and congenial as possible for the donor. A user-friendly bounce-back device—and by this I mean a pre addressed and maybe even postage-paid business reply envelope-should always be a part of your receipt "package." I will not enter into the broadly debated question about the implications of postage-paid versus donor-supplies-the-stamp envelopes. There are sound arguments for both sides of the issue.

Current Giving Program

"Current Giving Program" refers to all of the activities and events in which you are presently engaged that produce income. There are two major issues at stake here. The first is whether these current giving programs are looked upon as merely sources for current revenue or whether they are indeed also looked upon as a source for prospecting for the "lift" project, as in, "win, keep, lift." The other issue, at least eventually, ought to be whether these events should be continued indefinitely.

A Christian school I worked with once concluded that most of its events were not cost-effective and that most should be discontinued in favor of allocating money and energy for other things within the IFDS model that would produce more income for less financial outlay and would create a better image and better donor relations.

It is very easy to look upon current gift projects only with regard to the net proceeds from the event. Of course we need money now for ongoing expenses. But it becomes very easy in the heat of the moment and the urgency of need to forget that current income projects ought also to be utilized for the purpose of causing donors to increase their participation as partners.

An easily overlooked element of current giving programs has to do with the image the organization projects of itself by the event. Do you want your public to think of you in the context of auctions, candy bar sales, and other nickel and dime type events? Or, would you prefer that they think of you as highly professional and thoughtful in your fundraising endeavors? Also, when people give small gifts as a result of a sale or auction, you may well be forfeiting the opportunity to relate to them professionally so as to inspire them to give larger amounts.

In summary, you must be absolutely ruthless in the assessing of your current giving activities. Are the events projecting precisely the kind of image you desire? Are you following through on every event to ensure maximum participation by donors rather than minimum, token participation? Are the events indeed cost-effective? In measuring event response, are you looking at the net income or only the gross income?

The Multi-Year Sustained Program

Current giving programs are designed for smaller gifts to build a large base of contributors. This base of small-gift contributors becomes a prospect pool for multi-year sustained gift contributors. When an individual makes a gift of $100 or more, he or she qualifies as a prospect for the Multi-Year Sustained Program.

The sustained gift program must be presented face-to-face with prospects for a number of reasons:

1. The complexity of the commitment which is sought.

2. The contributor's interest level can be determined only in a personal interview.

3. To evaluate whether the contributor is a major gift or deferred gift prospect.

The Multi-Year Sustained Program is designed as a club program in which contributing members commit to give a set amount annually, quarterly, or monthly with no termination unless canceled in writing. Contributors select the level of giving from various options within the program.

There are many benefits associated with the multi-year-sustained approach:

1. The contributors are sustained over a period of years, reducing the organization's annual fundraising costs.

2. It provides a predictable income stream.

3. It involves face-to-face contact that builds a relationship between the organization and the contributor.

4. It identifies prospects for capital gifts or a planned or deferred gift.

5. It provides for the gathering of contributor data.
6. It facilitates a way of identifying leadership for the organization's capital campaigns, projects, and even board membership.
7. It encourages contributor retention.
8. It provides a method of soliciting referrals.

The Multi-Year Sustained Program deepens the relationship with the donors, strengthens that friendship, and enables the organization to show appreciation in a way that cannot be accomplished in any other manner. An important ingredient of this program is the board's taking action, requesting that the staff, for example, enlist 500 people to be members of the President's Circle, or whatever you choose to call your program. The person doing the presentation can then say that the board has requested that these multi-year-sustained members be recruited so that the organization can more accurately plan its future activities in the light of these sustained gifts.

Joining this kind of club raises the donor's sense of belonging in a way that few other devices afford. Some kind of recognition tool can be utilized here in the form of an inexpensive plaque or certificate identifying the donor as a member of this club.

One of the most important strategies I have discovered with regard to the multi-year program is to first ask privately (one-on-one) each and every board member to become a part of this sustained-giving endeavor. Also, every staff member should then be solicited. Next, every volunteer who is assisting in the ministry should be asked to join. It is powerful to tell prospective club members that your entire board and staff have joined this effort. Only then should you branch out to others in your donor base.

A sure prescription for failure in the multi-year effort is to ask the board as a group to make these presentations. There is very little likelihood that everyone on any board will be able and/or willing to do this kind of work. Indeed, you as the development officer or CEO might well recruit board members to help but it should be done on an individual basis and not as a group.

Another key component of this program is the "lift" device. Remember that you are always assuming that if people are already giving to your organization at a certain level, then if they are able and if the Lord leads them, they might well wish to increase their giving.

In making these presentations to people, you will encounter every imaginable kind of response. Remember, these people are already donors; they are already friends of the organization. Many will be glad to commit themselves to giving regularly until they choose to cancel in writing. Others will have responses that diverge widely, and if you do this long enough and make enough presentations, you will run into still more unusual responses that you couldn't have imagined. It is important that you never argue, pressure, or coerce. You are merely there offering them this opportunity for further involvement with the organization.

One important lesson I have learned in making these presentations is never to leave the ball in the donor's court. Often, people will tell you that they want to pray about this matter, or they will say that they need time to think it over. It is critical at this point that you ask whether you might call them at some specific future time to inquire about their answer. The point is to ensure that you are leaving the decision entirely to them, but that you will take the initiative to follow up with them.

Another important result of the multi-year presentation to existing donors is the information you are able to gather concerning the donor. Let's consider our Mr. Smith again: you will be able discern his potential for future involvement as a result of your conversation with him. You may well discover that Mr. Smith is a prospect for a planned or deferred gift. Or, Mr. Smith may indicate in some way that he might be interested in participating in a future capital campaign. You may learn the Mr. Smith would make a volunteer in your work.

It is imperative that once you leave the company of Mr. Smith, you record immediately the information about this donor that you have gleaned. (The really good professional sales people of the business world have been doing this on call sheets and contact reports for ages; they know that the more they know about their customers, the better they can serve them.) Whether you jot this data down on a card or enter it on your laptop, be sure you do it right away, before vital facts slip out of your memory. Then, your impressions and discoveries need to become a part of the donor's file back at your office. This will ensure that other development colleagues-present and future-will be able to acquaint themselves with these facts.

Capital Campaigns

A capital campaign can be a valuable tool for providing resources to expand or strengthen your ministry. Properly organized and executed, it can generate income that may never otherwise be given to your organization. However, it must be well planned and researched or the campaign could have a negative effect upon your ministry. The timing, project needs, and organization stability are all-important factors in planning for a capital campaign.

A major capital campaign requires a well-defined and segmented mailing list and cash reserves to finance the campaign until the given income stream becomes a reality. Be sure to build into the campaign budget all the costs of conducting the campaign.

Cash reserves and a steady income stream are needed to fund important pre-campaign work and adequate development systems. Costs may include computerization, specialized development software, mailing list segmentation, and the writing and production of printed materials, consultant's fees, and various other projects leading to the capital campaign.

It has become a truism among consultants leading capital campaigns that major contributors tend to give more than 80 percent of the campaign gifts. Approximately 80 percent of the contributors give the remaining 20 percent of the goal. The importance of the small contributor group, however, cannot be overstated. While the majority of the work in a capital campaign is with the small contributor group and has a distorted cost/benefit ratio, these people are extremely important to future campaigns.

Several benefits are realized by the extensive work done with the 80% small contributor group:

1. The 80-percent group will usually produce sufficient income to cover campaign expenses.

2. The extensive public relations campaign builds a strong foundation for the next campaign, usually to be launched in three years.

3. The volunteers enlisted for this part of the campaign may provide key leadership in future campaigns.

4. The larger market position impact is vital for future funding.

It is extremely rare for an organization's staff and board to plan and execute a capital campaign in-house. Undoubtedly someone reading this will know of an exception. Indeed, there are a few exceptions. Most staffers simply do not have the experience and expertise to execute a capital campaign. Hiring a reputable consulting company to lead your campaign is the best money you will ever spend.

Volunteers who have been trained by a competent consultant should perform the laborious tasks inevitable in a capital campaign. Otherwise, the training and execution of tasks will fall on the shoulders of your staff, thus creating a sometimes-fatal disruption of the work that the organization exists to perform.

The importance of a feasibility study as a prelude to a capital campaign cannot be overemphasized. I recently had an interesting conversation with a bright, young executive of a ministry in Ohio. His ministry's total budget was under $300,000 with a mere $78,000 in the form of contributions. He, his staff and board launched a $2.1 million capital campaign three months prior to our discussion. There had been no feasibility study whatsoever, just the sincere hope that they could raise the money for a much-needed facility. I was not at all surprised to learn that only $24,000 had come in toward the $2.1 million goal. No matter what public relations spin you put on a situation like this, the organization appears in the minds of its constituency to be a failure. A feasibility study would have prevented this embarrassment.

First, outsiders who are competent and experienced should conduct a feasibility study. The development company you hire to do your feasibility study will personally interview anywhere from 25 to 200 people from your constituency, depending upon the size of your donor base. These personal interviews will include major donors, board members, former board and former staff, community political leaders, and selected individuals within the community power structure. These interviews will be characterized by the assurance of anonymity and confidentiality.

The feasibility study will not only tell you accurately how much money is available for a proposed project; it will provide you with answers to any questions you devise. Then, the same questionnaire used in the face-to-face interviews will be mailed to the entire donor base as well as other selected community leaders. Their responses will be returned in a postage-paid reply envelope to the consulting firm's officers, where all the data will be tabulated and analyzed and compiled into a report.

A feasibility study will give you information that will be helpful in preparing for a capital campaign as well as overall future ministry. The obvious benefit is that you will know precisely how much money is available to you for this specific project over a three-year period. But you will learn much more than just how much money might be available. A feasibility study will tell you what your constituents and community leaders think about your organization, the timing of the capital campaign, and its relevance in the light of the community's needs overall.

I have heard from numerous sources the expression of sincere regret that they launched a capital campaign without doing their homework: a feasibility study. I cannot recall ever hearing anyone lament about having conducted such a study.

Planned and Deferred Gifts

One of the most important lessons regarding development you can ever learn is that information and relationships drive all large gifts. Nowhere does this fact become more evident than in the realm of planned and deferred gifts. We can all remember tales of organizations benefiting to the tune of many hundreds of thousands of dollars as a result of a legacy. All of us who have headed up ministries have fantasized at one time or another about our organization becoming the beneficiary of such a gift. Rarely does this kind of gift come about apart from a long-standing relationship.

Perhaps a few simple definitions will help at this point. My dear friend Robert F. Sharpe defines a planned gift as "any gift given in any amount, given for any purpose-operations, capital expansion, or endowment—whether for current or deferred use, which requires the assistance of a professional staff person, a qualified volunteer, or the donor's advisors to complete. In addition, it includes any gift which is carefully considered by a donor in the light of estate and financial plans."

A deferred gift is simply a planned gift that has a delayed benefit to the charity. Usually the death of the contributor precedes the realization of the gift.

An annuity is a fixed sum, payable periodically, subject to the limitations of the grantor—generally, either for life or for a number of years. In a charitable gift annuity, a specified percent of the gift is paid back to the contributor for life.

A trust is an entity that holds assets for the benefit of certain other persons or entities. The person holding legal title or interest, who has responsibility for the assets and for the distribution of the assets or the distribution of the income generated by such assets, is the trustee.

While there can be exceptions, it is generally true that a prospect for planned giving is a person who has a strong interest in your ministry and a meaningful relationship with its leaders, who is 60 years of age or more, who is concerned about capital gains or estate tax problems, who is a current significant financial supporter of your ministry, who has some appreciated assets, perhaps has holdings of real estate, and has stock or other types of securities. He or she very often will be a person who has no children but needs additional income. You might surface such a prospect by hearing him express a need for help with estate or tax planning.

An immediate gift is one of the planned giving options your donor might consider. This may include real estate, artwork, antiques, stocks, bonds, or other securities. Also included might be life loans and charitable lead trusts. Another option would be deferred gifts, which might include wills and revocable trusts, gift annuities and charitable remainder trusts. Charitable remainder trusts might include annuity trusts, unitrusts and wealth replacement trusts. In addition there might be pooled income funds and life insurance.

Many sophisticated organizations today are conducting estate planning seminars for selected donors among their constituencies. These kinds of presentations are usually more effective with small groups of six to ten couples and should be by invitation only. The ministry representative, usually the CEO or the development officer, should lead the estate planning session but should also include a competent attorney who is sympathetic to the ministry and a certified financial planner.

Since these pages are intended for the novice in the field of development, you might be grappling with the question of how to begin to do the work of planned and deferred gifts. The first and most obvious place to start is with selected members of your donor base. Provide them information concerning wills, tactfully advising them of how they might remember your organization in their wills. Purchasing commercially prepared "Wills" leaflets that can be imprinted with your organization's name, logo, and address can do this very professionally.

As you become more savvy in your involvement with planned and deferred giving, you will want to rely heavily on the many individuals and organizations across the country that specialize in advising Christian organizations in these very matters. These people can be of great benefit to you in your early stages, long before you are ready to put a full time person on your staff who would devote all his or her attention to planned and deferred giving.

Who's in Charge of Fund Raising?

It is easy to point a finger and assign blame when it comes to responsibility for funding the organization. Many times we have heard the CEO blame the board for the lack of funds. There are surely as many instances where the board blames the CEO and other staffers for funding insufficiencies.

There exists no more commonly recurring problem than that of the CEO's high expectations of the board (and the board's expectations of the CEO) regarding their responsibility in fund raising. Steven Covey was right when he wrote that all frustration is the result of expectations.

Board members give and raise money for the same reasons anyone else gives: values, awareness, priority. It is unreasonable to expect that board members will give just because they have been made board members. Likewise, development expertise will seldom be present in a board when it does not exist first in the CEO. I doubt that there has ever been a board that was consistently effective in giving and raising money when the CEO did not mentor them.

Let's see if we can address some of the issues that confront us here.

First, *no one should be a member of a board who does not give and does not encourage others to give.* There can be no question but that the board of any charitable organization bears the brunt ultimately for financial accountability. This is referred to as fiduciary responsibility. However, to interpret that to mean that the board must become expert in the art, skill, and science of the procurement of funds in our culture borders on the ridiculous. Active and willing? Yes! Expert? No.

Individuals who happen to serve on boards give for the same reasons that anyone else gives. If we cajole board members to give money to an organization simply because they serve on the board, when in reality they are not committed enough to the values of the organization to give voluntarily and cheerfully, then they should not be on the board at all.

I once served an organization that had a board of 31 people and not a single one had given a contribution to the ministry for several years. That is obviously very wrong. If a person is going to assume the responsibility of boardsmanship, he or she must be willing to give and the reason for giving ought to go far beyond the simple fact that he or she is a board member.

Board members must be cultivated as donors just like all other people. Mind you, board members should be asked to give to the ministry, but they should first be asked as individuals as far as motive is concerned, and as board members only from a secondary point of view. If a person does not really have a heart for the ministry, then that person should never under any circumstances serve as a board member. Indeed, the very first requirement for board membership ought always to be an unqualified embracing of the cause for which the organization exists.

While the board has ultimate fiduciary responsibility, it is the CEO and his/her staff who are ultimately responsible for development. The CEO should be held accountable solely by the board of directors. When a CEO steps aside from the responsibility for the financial health of the organization, he is abdicating one of his most serious roles. Yet, this happens repeatedly. Most often, I suspect, it is done because the CEO is more interested in doing the work for which the organization exists than managing and ensuring that a healthy development process is in place.

The very first hurdle for the CEO of a ministry is to accept his or her biblical role in fund raising. One of the most subtle traps to which a leader can succumb is to pit ministry against fund raising. The Bible could not possibly be more clear than when it shows us that giving money in order that the gospel might go forth is the very clear design of God Himself. God, in His omnipotence, could have devised any imaginable, or unimaginable to us, manner of financing His work, but He ordained that it should be by the means of giving. Therefore, to relegate to a secondary position the procuring of funds for ministry is to go against the clear teachings of Scripture. In my long tenure in ministry and charitable giving, I cannot remember an organization being successful in the procurement of money when there was an absence of expertise in development on the part of the leadership and staff. And yet, so many ministry leaders continue to blame the lack of funds on the board.

The term most widely used today to refer to the work an organization does to secure funds for ministry is the word *development*. Let there be no question about it: successful development requires a great deal of knowledge. Yet, every day of the week, someone is hired as development director for a para-church ministry because he or she has been a successful pastor, insurance salesperson, possesses a marketing degree or has a great love for the ministry and wants to serve the Lord. There could be many reasons for the hiring of an individual, but no one should even be considered for development work unless he or she has a grasp of development and the personality to enable him or her to learn and to grow in the knowledge of this kind of ministry.

Development is a full-time ministry. With the exception of a few retired persons devoting their services to boards, most board members are volunteers and many have extreme time limitations imposed upon them by their work and families. This in itself makes it quite unreasonable to put undue and unbearable responsibility on the board for development work. The board's job is not to write case statements, maintain donor records, write letters, manage the mailing lists, etc. Board members are responsible for friend and fund raising through their respective networks in the community, according to their gifts and abilities. Yes, they must be willing participants, but their part of the process must be facilitated and made easy by the professional staff, so that the time they can give to the task is used wisely and effectively. Generally, this translates to introducing the CEO and giving him or her access to key people of means and to one-on-one visits with prospects—not deep-into-the-night committee meetings, manning telephone banks, or writing grant proposals.

If there is a development committee, it assists the staff alone and should never be a committee of the board, although selected board members might be invited to serve on the committee. When it comes to development, we should look to the board for help, but not expect that it will be expert in the science and art of development. Professionals skilled in the field must guide development, with the CEO riding point at all times.

The staff should have its own committees selected at large and based upon the expertise sought. Think of the development committee as a task force with a specific mission. The staff person responsible, either the director of development or the CEO, should chair it. As a task force, it should be ad hoc and never a standing committee in nature. It is an advisory body and therefore does not make decisions as a group. No minutes are kept.

Does this mean board members are off the hook? Never! The board is ultimately responsible for the financial health and integrity of the organization. As good stewards, there should be keen interest on the part of all the directors in the development process.

The board assesses the health of the funding of the organization through its monitoring of the CEO alone. In an attempt to fulfill its fiduciary role the board often delves into the details of the budget and development.

Warning: The board should never meddle in the details as it will quickly lose sight of the ends. Keep focused on the vision.

The wise board will look to the CEO alone for information with regard to the organization's health. The board will use whatever means necessary to monitor the organization through the CEO and hold him or her accountable. Just as the board speaks with a single voice or not at all, so the board should hear officially from a single person: the CEO. If performance is lacking, the board must deal with the CEO either through a restatement of its expectations coupled with a defined period of time within which these are to be achieved, or through direct removal from office.

The ideal situation is experienced when there is harmonious and dedicated teamwork between staff and board with regard to development. We would all agree that teamwork can only take place when it is clear to all concerned what each party's role is. In this team of staff and board, there is no question but that the board has final fiduciary responsibility and must monitor the performance of the staff with regard to the results of development efforts. But it should be equally clear that the responsibility for the development strategy and implementation belongs solely to the staff. What does not move the organization forward is the board member who roars in off the freeway, his or her cellular phone in use, rushing apologetically late into a board meeting only to give knee-jerk advice fifteen minutes later on a subject about which he or she knows very little. *(Isn't it interesting how people will steer clear of offering advice to the pastor on how to preach his sermon, but will think nothing of undertaking the design of the organization's public relations strategy or a major funding campaign? Why is it that everyone is a marketing expert?)*

On the other hand, the teamwork is greatly enhanced if the board advises and assists the efforts of the staff in every way possible. It is a fact that peers can better tell the professional how to approach major donor prospects because they live, work and play together. More often they know these prospects infinitely better than does the CEO or the development director.

The greatest contribution the board can make to development is to ensure vision. The effective board of directors is constantly looking outside of the organization—at the fulfillment, or lack thereof, of the organization's vision. The board spends its time addressing the needs that exist and what good will be brought about in the world as a result of the organization's ministry. Traditionally, boards tend to look inside their organizations more frequently than they look outside. The word *ends* is used to describe the task of boards rather than goals or objectives because the board will have its own goals and objectives, as will the staff, to do its work. The goals for the board will be considerably different from the goals of the staff. The ends, which the board addresses primarily, are the *results* toward which the staff's efforts are directed.

It is only when the board sticks strictly to *ends* issues, rather than *means*, that it can articulate the good for which the organization exists to bring about. This is the most important single contribution to funding the board can make.

CHAPTER 13

Development & the Local Church

"There is no more infallible barometer of spiritual health than how people spend money."

Differences

Most of us in ministry have assumed that development, as practiced in para-church ministries, has nothing to do with local church funding. I have come to believe that the church can learn from the development specialists in para-church organizations. To be sure, there are some differences.

Teaching Versus Value-Matching

Traditionally, we have thought of the church as featuring stewardship and the para-church as being involved in development. True, the church is the place for teaching what the Bible has to say about giving. The para-church organization has little if any platform for such teaching. There is neither time nor opportunity for such teaching. The para-church is simply looking for donors whose values match the values of the ministry of the organization. The local church aims at getting its message to everybody in its constituency. The para-church should not expect that every Christian will be interested in giving to its causes.

On the other hand, the local church should expect that every member will give to its programs and causes. The para-church can always move on to another audience: its members and attendees. If I don't give to my church, there is no one else to whom the church can appeal. It is unrealistic to presume that the person in another church across town will give to *my* church.

Once we understand the differences between the para-church and the local church, the task is to devise a strategy that fosters giving.

Annual Emphasis and Pledging

One of my favorite stories concerns a church in Memphis. The pastor of a Presbyterian church there picked up the local paper one morning to learn that one of his fellow-elders had given a million dollars to a nearby college. He immediately went to the telephone and called the man. He asked why that million dollars had not been given to the church. The explanation was that the college had asked for a gift and the church had not.

The people of our church need to be asked to give, taught to give, and treated with care as donors.

Many pastors boast that they never teach concerning money. This assumes that our people are not only sanctified but perhaps even glorified! Should we not consider stewardship a part of "the whole counsel of God"? The New Testament is replete with teachings and admonitions regarding money. To avoid the subject as pastors is to do so at our own peril. And at the peril of our people.

We need not only ask our people to give to the local church, we need to admonish, encourage and make it rewarding for them to do so. Most churches that are successful in funding have some kind of annual teaching and emphasis on the subject. This is usually a time when not only the giving of money is spotlighted, but also the stewardship of all of life. Often an entire month is set aside for biblical teaching on the subject.

I cannot overemphasize the importance of culminating this teaching with the asking of your people to respond, to make a commitment. Use every God-honoring device at your disposal to move your people from "hearing" to "doing" the Word of God.

In the early days of my ministry I learned of the faith promise system devised by the renowned Toronto pastor, J. Oswald Smith. Years later I would speak at a missions conference in his church, then pastored by his son, Paul. Also, I became a friend of the man who would write the book describing Smith's faith promise system. Thousands of churches around the world have used the Smith method of raising money for missions. The strategy is simple: teach the Word of God regarding missions, ask the people to make a promise to give, and then trust God to provide. Some variation of this strategy should be implemented in every church: teach and ask.

Welcoming New Donors

Through the years my wife, Libby, and I have moved from city to city and therefore have attended many new churches. Whenever I have put in the offering plate our first check I have wondered if anyone noticed that we were new givers. Apparently, no one ever did notice. I always wondered why someone didn't write to us acknowledging that we had given our first contribution and thanking us and perhaps telling us something of how the money is used and what the church's vision is.

Technology makes it possible, even easy, to detect new givers and provide them with a warm welcome. Para-church organizations that practice good development do this routinely. Why don't churches?

The surest fact about donors is that we're going to lose some. They *are* going to die, move away, lose their jobs, or just get mad at the pastor. We are going to lose donors. This same technology makes it possible to know when people stop giving. The regrettable part is that the technology will not intervene for us to find out why they stopped giving and discover if something can be done to fix the problem.

Welcoming new donors and intervening on behalf of lapsed donors makes sense. It is the gracious thing to do. These two steps could increase your church income more than you can imagine. Plus, these measures build bridges for good relationships and ministry opportunities.

Reporting

Most churches I have observed do little by way of reporting to givers. Some display the weekly budget and income, along with the overage or deficit in the weekly bulletin. While this is better than nothing, it is far from adequate for donor cultivation and motivation.

Again, technology is our friend in the work of development. With the right software you can now send a quarterly report that is personalized, showing the amount an individual has pledged and the amount given. This affords you another opportunity to thank them for their gifts and once again do the vital work of vision casting. It is impossible to thank donors too often or to restate your mission, vision, and goals too often.

The research of one of my clients revealed that on average their donors were giving to seven ministries in addition to their church. Many of the para-church organizations are expert at asking and reporting to donors. The church can ill afford to do less.

Planned and Deferred Giving

I recently was visiting with a para-church director of development who told me his institution received an average of two legacies per week! I have never been able to understand why the local church leaves most planned-giving harvesting to the para-church organization.

Many denominations have stewardship people who are specialists in this field and available to assist churches in this vital work. While they do not always take my advice, I urge all local churches where I am consulting to have at least two or three estate planning events each year. The greatest transfer of wealth in the history of mankind is taking place now, at the turn of the century. The Depression-era people who found they could not spend the money they accumulated are coming to the end of their lives. This is a great opportunity to help people determine before they die where their money will go.

I repeatedly encounter two fatal assumptions regarding this matter. One is the assumption that because people in a particular church are not wealthy there is little need for estate planning. We think that because people live in a modest house and drive ten-year-old cars they have no estate worth mentioning. Maybe not! Remember, the people of the Depression-era often find it difficult to spend money, no matter how much they have accumulated.

The second assumption is that everyone already has a will and an estate plan. Again, not so. I often ask my audiences how many of them have wills. To my dismay, easily half say they do not.

Never-Ending Capital Campaigns

I have a pastor friend in California who told me he was starting his seventh three-year capital campaign in just over 20 years of service to that congregation. Conversely, pastors can't wait for the end of a capital campaign. A financially healthy church will always be in the midst of or preparing for a capital campaign.

Look at it this way: as long as there are needs to be met, people to be reached, missions to be accomplished, we should be offering people the opportunity to give. Also, your people are always coming into possession of new funds through inheritance, promotions, sale of assets, bonus and commission payments, etcetera. Furthermore, since you started your present campaign you have brought in many new people. They need the chance to participate, too.

When you think of the stewardship work of your church, think not only of the annual emphasis, usually at year's end, but also think of estate planning and capital campaigns. All three are essential elements of a financially healthy church.

Endowments

A pastor friend of mine was told by one of his members that he had one million dollars he wanted to give to the church. My very wise friend graciously told the man that he could not allow that to happen. He explained that it would endanger the giving of other members. Very wise! He did tell the man he would welcome $60,000 to redo the parking lot and $200,000 for an endowment to cover the cost of maintenance of the buildings. He also offered to help the man select some missions, colleges and seminaries to which he might give.

It seems wise to me to always build into a capital campaign an endowment for the upkeep of buildings. Beyond that, endowments for a local church can be dangerous.

The sheep of your pasture deserve your shepherding them fully, even including money.

CHAPTER 14

Governance/ Boardsmanship

"Governance is more than management writ large"

—John Carver[1]

There is Hope for Boards

A leader in Seattle said, "This Carver model for boards puts awful responsibility on me as CEO!" He is right! But it also puts great responsibility upon the board. However, the spheres are totally different. The board's role is governance; the staff's role is management. Until these two areas of work are clearly differentiated there will be paralyzing confusion and conflict.

There is probably more management information available concerning boards than any single management subject. The problem is that almost all the literature deals with the traditional model for board work. To the best of my knowledge, only John Carver has devised a totally new model for board work in not-for-profit organizations. He describes this in his excellent book, *Boards That Make a Difference*.

Carver limits the work of boards to only four categories:

1. Ends

2. Executive Limitations

3. Board/Staff Relationships

4. Board Process

These areas and only these areas comprise governance. Everything else is management and thus belongs to the staff. Almost all board problems can be traced to the confusion of governance with management.

If the solution to so many of our board/staff difficulties is so obvious, then why are so many organizations so slow to adopt the Carver model? The answer is *tradition*.

The Robert's Rules of Order parliamentary model has been with us for over 100 years. (Henry Martyn Robert was called on to preside at a meeting in 1860 while he was a cadet at West Point. Because he did not know how to conduct a meeting and did so poorly, he determined to put in writing what he subsequently learned. In essence, his writings were the adaptation of the rules of Congress to meet the needs of all types of organizations.)

A Baptist pastor in Texas defended the continued use of Robert's model because Robert was a Baptist! I don't think that's reason enough. We need a whole new model for board work.

Your board may well be made up of good people with good intentions and noble commitment to the organization. However, if the model for their work is flawed, their good qualities may well be nullified.

Likewise, your CEO and other staff may be good people who are expected to rise above the flaws of traditional board/staff structures. We all can remember instances of good staff people, especially CEOs, who have been destroyed by an ancient model that doesn't work.

There is hope for your board! In recent years I have presented this policy governance model to ministries all across the country with amazing results. While it certainly is not a cure-all, it surely is the best hope I have come upon for the quagmire in which many boards are snared.

Peter Drucker says, "All nonprofit boards have one thing in common. They do not work."

He is right, but there is hope. The starting point for hope is to clearly separate governance from everything else in ministry.

The Pathology of Nonprofit Boards

Here are warning signs that a board may be improperly focusing on the management side versus governance issues:

- Micro-managing staff work
- Rubber-stamping staff decisions
- Consuming precious time with trivial matters
- Responding only to staff situations and initiatives—being reactive rather than proactive
- Not clarifying board/staff gray areas
- Assuming that either less or more involvement will solve board problems
- Failing to distinguish governance from management
- Expecting board committees to assist with staff work

Sorting Out the Roles of Board & Staff

As I walked across the parking lot toward my rental car to head back to my hotel, my mind was filled with thoughts of déjà vu. I had just completed two days of interviews with senior and middle management staff and board members of a ministry that had come into existence soon after the end of World War II. I was struck once again with the fact that our problems in ministry are much more similar than dissimilar.

I cannot remember how many formal and informal management audits I have performed for ministries over the past 45 years, but one thing is sure—while no two ministries are exactly the same, to say the least, the problems that ministries face are easily predictable.

The ministry I had just left was characterized by serious and debilitating confusion with regard to board/staff relationships and roles, the role of the CEO in relation to other senior staff, and confusion with regard to the roles and authority of board committees. My mind went back over the long history of this ministry and I could not help being impressed with how God has used this work through the years. But I kept wondering how much more effective they might have become had they addressed the management problems with objectivity, knowledge of management, and courage to act.

The Role of the Board Is Governance

I suspect there is more information available with regard to nonprofit boards than any other single management subject, including fund raising. Unfortunately, all of the books, videos, audiotapes and seminars, including seminars I have taught for many years, merely provide tips on how to perform traditional board work. To the best of my knowledge only John Carver has come up with an all-new model for boardsmanship in the nonprofit organization.

When I came upon John Carver's book, *Boards That Make a Difference,* I went to my files and threw away everything I had collected on the subject of boards. Carver not only reinforced many of my beliefs concerning boards/staff relationships; he also provided a total framework for how boards might operate with a great reduction of friction and frustration. Carver calls his system *"Policy Governance"* or *"Governance by Design."* His approach is absolutely revolutionary! Even a casual reading of Carver will convince one that this is not a series of tips on how to do traditional board work but a total redesigning of the approach.

Simply put, boards have only four areas with which to deal: ends, board process, board/staff relationships and executive limitations. Let's take a moment and look at these four categories in depth.

The first is **ENDS**. Here the board deals simply with what good? for whom? and at what cost?

This means that the board's primary focus is outside the organization, addressing the needs that exist and what good will be brought about in the world as a result of the organization's ministry. Traditionally, organizations tend to look inside the organization more frequently than they look outside. The word *ends* is used to describe the task of boards rather than goals or objectives because the board will have its own goals and objective, as will the staff. The goals for the board will be considerably different from the goals of the staff. However, the ends, which the board primarily addresses, are the results to which the staff's efforts are focused.

Second, **BOARD PROCESS** is where the board states its own rules for how it will perform its work. Here the board determines how it will pursue consensus, how it will deal with renegade board members, how it will make decisions and how it will structure itself as a board.

One of the things the board must deal with in *board process* is its utilization of committees. The operative rule is that the board should keep a minimum number of committees and be absolutely ruthless in determining whether there should be any committee structure at all. If the board finds that committees are needed, it should ensure that these committees assist the board in doing its work. Boards can and should govern, but there is no way boards can or should, as a board, help the staff do its work.

In *board process*, the board determines its structure. In traditional board work there are any number of board officers created, whether needed or not. Minimalism is the rule of thumb for officers of a board. There should never be a board officer unless there is a need for that office to help the board do its own work.

The third area is **BOARD/STAFF RELATIONSHIPS**. This category considers how the board passes power to the staff, and determines how it will assess staff performance and how it will relate to the staff as a board.

Also, the board needs to be very specific in how it will assess the performance of the staff and particularly that of the CEO. The board should make it clear that just as the board speaks with one voice or not at all, so the board hears officially from the staff through one person or not at all. Of course, this does not mean that the CEO cannot call upon a staff member to give a report of significance to the board.

The fourth area of board work is **EXECUTIVE LIMITATIONS**. Carver explains that this means the board states negatively what it expects of the staff—that is, what it will not allow in staff performance. Almost always executive limitations deal with matters of ethics and prudence. Here is where the board articulates clearly what it will not allow in personnel relationships, budgeting, borrowing of money, putting assets at risk, relationships with vendors, and any other matters the board might specify. No single ingredient of this revolutionary way of doing board work gives greater freedom to the staff and reduces frustration more than this category of executive limitations.

As I have taught this principle over the past years, people sometimes suggest it might be a mistake to state these conditions negatively. Not so! Executive limitations are meant to place a fence around the very specific actions regarding ethics and prudence that the board will not allow. When executive limitations are stated negatively, it has a very positive effect on staff performance, for it frees the staff to do the job they were hired to do.

Traditional board work is characterized by a confusion of board/staff roles, obsession with details at the expense of the big picture, focusing on the short term rather than the long term, and being overwhelmed with volumes of information, resulting in frustration for both board and staff. When board and staff consider the Carver model, there are some legitimate questions that surface early on. Will the board lose control? Is it legal? Is it biblical and spiritual? What will people think? Will it help or hinder the staff? Why do we need to change the way we have been doing board work? A careful consideration of the Carver model will provide legitimate and satisfying answers to these kinds of questions.

Mind you, the Carver model will not compensate for an incompetent CEO or substitute for moral courage by the board, and indeed, it will not work if not implemented.

The Role of the CEO Is Management

Alan Weiss said in *Our Emperors Have No Clothes*, "The worst calamity in nonprofit management is a confusion (my kids would say they are clueless) about strategy and operational distinctions. Sit in on any number of management meetings, in any size operation, and you will find no distinction between the 'what' of direction and the 'how' of implementation. Yet in that simple difference is a profound tool for management."[2]

> Most organizations come into existence with the CEO as the visionary and the board as little more than a rubber stamp. In organizations that outlive the founder, boards often move to a position of micro-management.

The board's task is governance. The CEO's task is management. Confuse the two, and you dilute both.

People don't manage effectively for only two reasons. Either they don't know how, or they lack the will.

Recently, I spent two days

with a CEO and was hard pressed to suggest a management book that he had not read. And yet his management work was a disaster, and he was on the verge of being expelled from the organization. During my summary follow-up, I pointed out that he surely had the knowledge of management, but lacked the will and courage to act.

Aristotle said that all of our difficulty comes from our failure to define terms. He may have been right! It is imperative to adequately define management and ensure that the board stays out of all management activities. The best definition I have found is from Lawrence A. Appley's little publication, *Management Made Simple*, where he writes, "Simply put, management is the work we do to get work done through other people." The best description of management that I have come upon is from Louis A. Allen when he says that management consists of planning, leading, organizing, and controlling.

Planning is the work we do, says Allen, to predetermine a course of action. Planning consists of forecasting, establishing objectives, programming, scheduling, budgeting, establishing procedures and developing policies.

Organizing is the work we do to put people and tasks together in a structure. It consists of creating a structure, delegating responsibilities, developing job descriptions, and establishing and maintaining interpersonal human relationships.

Leading is the work we do which causes other people to take desired action. (John Maxwell's magnificent definition of leading is that it is simply influence.) Leading consists of making decisions, communicating, motivating, selecting the right people and developing them.

Controlling is the work we do to ensure that performance conforms to plan. It involves establishing standards, measuring performance, and correcting one's course as needed.

Space does not permit us to delve into the age-old question of the relationship between leading and managing. Louis Allen, and many other writers on management theory, make the role of leading as an essential function of management. Suffice it to say here that leadership without management is merely hype and inspiration. On the other hand, management without leadership is sterile and ineffective. Once you see that management involves a set of skills and a body of knowledge that can be acquired and implemented by almost anyone, there is hope for fulfilling the role of management.

Peter Drucker wrote, "An effective leader is not someone who is loved or admired. He or she is someone whose followers do the right things. Popularity is not leadership. Results are. Leaders are highly visible. They therefore set examples. Leadership is not rank, privileges, titles or money. It is responsibility."

Board leadership is different in essence and outcome from executive leadership. Boards should lead leaders, while the executive must lead both leaders and administrators.

The Role of Senior Staff Is Teamwork

"When a top executive is selecting his key associates, there are only two qualities for which he should be willing to pay almost any price: taste and judgment. Almost anything else can be bought by the yard."
—John Gardner

I once did a management audit for an organization that had the chief financial officer, program director and director of development reporting directly to the board. This created an impossible situation for the staff and the board, not to mention the CEO. You will not be surprised to hear that they had a long history of high turnover of both staff and board.

Senior staff is a part of the management process, not governance. They should report to the CEO. In turn, the CEO is held responsible by the board for the performance of the entire organization, including senior staff. Just as the board speaks to the organization through one person only, the CEO, so the board hears officially from the organization through only one person, the CEO.

The CEO may well invite senior staff to give reports to the board, answer the board's questions, and enjoy fellowship with the board, but they should never report to the board. Great care must be taken by the board in this process not to drift into the fatal error of giving orders to senior staff or appraising their work.

That task belongs to the CEO alone.

It is very common for boards to divide into committees, have a board member chair the committee, and work with a senior staff in his or her area. This approach to committee work almost never works. At best it creates hopeless bureaucracy, and at its worst it paralyzes staff and frustrates committee people.

If an organization is to have committees, they should be staff committees and never board committees. A staff person should chair the committee and should select his members based on their ability to contribute to a certain subject; the committee should never be made up of board members only. Indeed, a board member may well be selected to serve on a senior staff committee, but it should be because of his or her expertise and knowledge, and not because he or she is a board member.

There is every probability that the ministry you serve, as an executive or board member, faces very similar problems to the ones related here. It is my sincere hope that you might find the kernel of a few ideas that will help address these almost universal problems in Christian organizations.

Why Boards Can't Plan

A friend invited me to meet with him and his board chair. After the exchange of pleasantries, my friend explained that he would like me to conduct a retreat for his board and lead them through the process of strategic planning. I groped for ways to tell him that boards should not attempt to plan for organizations, that indeed, planning is a management tool, thus making it the distinct purview of staff. Boards can and should govern but they can never manage. To say it another way, boards can and should determine the ends for which organizations exist, but they should not attempt to prescribe the steps to reach those ends.

Not even adding the word *strategic* to planning makes it a viable board task. I can't remember when *strategic* became a buzzword to enhance planning. Now, many years and books later, I still can't figure why.

Planning is predetermining a course of action, throwing a net over tomorrow to cause to happen what we want to happen. It is clearly the work of the people who have day-to-day and hour-to hour control over what is happening. It is beyond the scope of board work.

Boards can define the target but they can't pull the bowstring.

All of this becomes credible when you distinguish between governance and everything else that goes on in the organization. Governance consists only of:

- determining the ends for which the organization exists,

- specifying what the staff may not do in the implementation of the means in pursuit of those ends,

- describing how the board relates to the staff through the CEO, and

- providing a set of rules for itself as a board.

Everything else is management and belongs to the staff.

There are at least four issues that should prevent boards from attempting the work of planning on behalf of the staff.

The task issue — No matter what you call it, planning is an inappropriate task for boards. To require that a board engage in planning is to ensure both frustration and failure. And, just as important, it lets the staff off the hook for performing a management task that is indispensable.

I have rummaged through my library and files in preparation for this chapter. Most of the material I looked at was idealistic, ethereal, and totally impractical. When theorists write about board planning, they seem to impute superhuman qualities to boards. Boards are not only human; they are busy and often detached from the organization. A board member recently confessed to me that he seldom thought of the organization until it was time for another meeting. Can you honestly expect that man to engage in planning?

The control issue — The work of planning involves implementing tasks that move a group of human beings toward a target, indeed a moving target. An activity that was useful yesterday might be irrelevant today, even counterproductive. Only if people are close to the tasks and empowered to make course corrections can we expect them to succeed.

In management, controlling is the work we do to ensure that performance conforms to the plan. Controlling often involves the hard work of making painful choices. This sometimes means we discipline staff, eliminate non-productive programs and realign budget allocations. A board that is removed from the action can't make these kinds of decisions.

The time issue — I once knew an organization that had a 31-person board made up entirely of retirees. The average age was 71 and the chairman was 91. They met every Friday at noon. Looking back, I suspect they were glad to have something to do. However, most boards are made up of busy people who have to make an effort to find time to attend a quarterly meeting. Incidentally, no board needs to meet monthly. To do so almost guarantees micro-management.

Planning is time-consuming. It requires constant evaluation of activities to ascertain that what we are doing is moving us toward the target the board specified.

The communications issue — Communication is the work we do to ensure understanding. Boards can expect to effectively communicate policy governance to the CEO but never can the board communicate means issues to a detached and diverse staff. In the policy governance model the board communicates with the staff only through one person: the CEO. A board can expect to create understanding with one person; it cannot expect to communicate on management issues to an entire staff.

Finally, I need to admit that boards should plan, but only for specific, codified board tasks, never for staff tasks. When boards attempt to plan for staff, it is almost always an effort to bolster an inept staff. This results in the board being diverted from governance and it never helps an incompetent staff.

It is almost impossible for boards to touch on organizational means without being seduced by the magnetism of details. It's like eating potato chips. Be prescriptive about staff means, just once, and you have to do it again and again.

A New Design for Committees

Few aspects of organizational life cause more frustration and waste more time than committees. At the same time, a group of people focused on a task can be a most valuable resource. The difference is in how the group is structured and how it operates.

The traditional committee is characterized by:

- bureaucracy,
- busyness,
- ineffectual compromise,
- inaction, and
- pursuit of personal agendas and confusion.

We need to redesign committees so they are characterized by:

- entrepreneurship,
- action,
- efficiency, and
- accomplishment.

This design will not only result in important work being accomplished but will bring satisfaction to the people involved.

We need to start with the fundamental question: Why do we have board committees? One, we want to put more minds to work on a problem or task in hopes of realizing the optimum solution. Two, we want to give board members ownership in the organization because, we reason, the more they participate, the more they will support and understand the organization.

The problem is that what happens is far different from the achievement initially hoped for by establishing the committee. Nowhere are committees more dangerous than when they are committees of the Board of Directors. One of two extremes usually sets in. More often than not, board committees assume the mantle of management and attempt to operate programs or staff functions. At the other end of the spectrum, social loafing takes root, albeit with every good intention. (Pamela Lewis, Stephen Goodman, and Patricia Fondt in their book, *Management*, define social loafing as "a tendency of people not to work as hard in groups as they would individually. This phenomenon occurs because their contribution is less noticeable and they are willing to let others carry the workload.")

An effective committee is not a device to keep board members informed and involved; staff reports serve this purpose. Neither should it be to give board members something "constructive" to do. The board members' focus on governance and *ends* ought not be diverted for any reason. Board dabbling in management and *means* can only result in confusion among staff, members, clients, and the community at large.

Traditional Committee Limitations

Most committee problems stem from our blind adherence to tradition. In the past we voted, kept minutes, and met without clear reasons; so we continue to do so. Not merely satisfied with the burdens of the past, we eagerly create new baggage as we go along.

1. Traditional committees are hopelessly bureaucratic. There is too much dependence on group decision making which limits a manager's ability to act quickly and decisively when necessary.

2. Traditional committees are caught up in the busyness of committee work: keeping unnecessary minutes, abiding by parliamentary rules designed for political debate, and maintaining a keen sense of perpetual self-importance.

3. Compromise reigns, resulting in ineffective decisions. Almost always, the results are not optimal for organizational effectiveness or performance.

4. Traditional committees work slowly. Often the problem has been resolved, or it has dissipated or annihilated the organization, before reaction has been defined.

5. Traditional committees, particularly board committees, seek to satisfy personal needs rather than the needs of the organization. Because board members of non-profit organizations donate their time and money, it is difficult not to let them exercise their personal agendas within committee meetings; even more problematic is when peers pander to these agendas and encourage non-issue-centered role-playing rather than issue-centered discussion.

6. Traditional committees always involve too many people, proving the veracity of Shanahand's Law: "The length of a meeting rises with the square of the number of people present."

7. Issues are never clearly focused and dealt with head-on for fear of offending opposing viewpoints within the committee. The usual escape is as described by Hartz's Law of Rhetoric: "Any argument carried far enough will end up in semantics."

The New Design for Committees

The guiding principle regarding committees is minimalism. An organization that is well managed and governed will generally find no need for any standing committee. No committees should be the starting point. A committee should not exist unless it is strategic, necessary, useful and helpful.

Assuming there really is legitimate cause for having a committee, let's consider seven rules for healthy committees to function.

1. Call it a task force rather than a committee — While it is true that words are only symbols, they are unbelievably important. We are much more apt to be able to get a group to function efficiently and effectively if we call the group a task force than if we call the group a committee. *Task force* suggests that there is work to be done and that there is some urgency and importance about it. It suggests that the group is a tactical unit with a beginning and an end. On the other hand, the word *committee* conjures up memories of long meetings and frustration in the midst of discussion with little being accomplished.

2. Be mission-specific — Clearly articulate the issue, problem, or task to be resolved. The more narrowly drawn the boundaries, the more focused will be the thinking and consideration of the group and the less likely they will be to stray into unrelated management areas.

3. Make it ad hoc—not standing—in nature — There are occasions when a committee may exist in perpetuity, but they are rare. Letting people know at the outset that they will be called together only when there is work to do is a powerful tool. It announces that you are sensitive to their time constraints and serious about accomplishment.

There are times when you may be required by an outside agency or association to have a standing committee, but this is unusual. Board committees should not be created with titles that in any way suggest a duplication of staff functions, because those committees will drift into staff work. Personnel, program, and finance committees all denote management functions. Oversight is easily achieved by the board *acting as a whole* in its review of organizational results. Oversight is not picking at nits, second-guessing the finance director or personnel manager.

4. Require that the person ultimately responsible for the work chair it — Tradition dictates that when a committee is formed, a chairperson is elected along with other officers. The staff person is considered as merely a resource person to the committee. This process only increases the layers in the organizational structure, resulting in the staff person having an additional boss. The committee becomes his or her supervisor as well as the staff person to whom he/she already reports. This violates the one-boss rule of good management.

We stand some chance of achieving results when delegating to an individual but never when delegating to a group. If the chairperson is the staff person to whom the work has been delegated and the committee is there to assist and advise only, we then have the best of both worlds. Groups should be for thinking...individuals are for action.

5. Insist it be non-decision-making in its role — Groups of humans are at their worst when they are making decisions and at their best when they are thinking, knowing in advance they will not be asked to decide.

Alex Osborne, who coined the term *brainstorming*, set down five rules for creative thinking in his classic, *Applied Imagination*. Rule number one is, "All judgment is suspended!"[3] He knew that groups could not be making decisions and be creative at the same time.

There is an old management adage that says the greatest opportunity for crisis comes at the point of group decision making. Removing decision making from the group maximizes the light and minimizes the heat. People are much freer to be creative and honest in their views if they know in advance they will not be called upon to take sides.

6. No rules, no minutes, no form — When a committee keeps minutes, it declares itself to be authoritative rather than advisory. There will be times when individuals may make notes of assignments and ideas, especially the chairperson. Notes as reminders can be helpful, whereas minutes tend to contribute to bureaucracy.

Parliamentary procedure has no place in a think tank. Rules stifle the imagination, forcing people's minds to consider form above function. These are times for brainstorming, not braindraining.

7. Keep the group small — Involve only those who can bring perspective, experience and talent to the issue. Why exacerbate the problem or issue by inviting lack of perspective, inexperience, and people with no relevant skills to search for the resolution? A wealthy donor does not an effective task-force member make! Reward and involve these people in other ways that are not detrimental to the mission of the organization.

Keep the number of people small. We suggest that you never exceed seven. This is the maximum number, it seems, beyond which social loafing, role-playing and all the negative baggage of group dynamics are set into motion.

The CEO Job Description

Recently I was invited to a very pleasant dinner by three board members from an East Coast non-profit organization. Initially the talk centered upon their organization's need to raise large sums of money for an expansion program and debt retirement. Soon, however, the focus shifted to the relationship of the CEO to the board.

The issues to me were familiar ones. Perhaps hundreds of times I had listened to this kind of discussion. Immediately evident was a deep frustration and confusion on the part of both the CEO and the board as to who is responsible to do what.

The board was in the process of writing a job description for the CEO. They were hoping that this exercise might resolve the difficulties that were producing the frustration and confusion that both the board and the CEO were experiencing.

As I sat there absorbing the now-familiar litany of issues of these concerned board members and knowing I would continue to hear of strikingly similar problems from a broad diversity of clients in the future, I thought to myself, *It's a good thing there is hope for this!*

When it was my turn to talk that evening, I gently reminded the men that the writing of a job description is not the purview of a board and to do so would inevitably draw them into operations of the organization and away from governance.

The task of the board is to prescribe the ends — the goals, the reason for being — of the organization, and then to entrust an individual (the CEO) with the daily management of the organization in the accomplishment of those ends. The board may specify the management devices it will use to assess progress, but must leave the rest up to the individual they have selected as CEO.

Boards should never measure or prescribe the activities of the CEO. Rather, the board should measure total organizational results. Boards should hold the CEO and the CEO alone responsible for results. The CEO in turn should be free to manage staff for results to ensure the accomplishment of board-specified ends.

The board is concerned with the *ends* for which the organization exists, not the management of *means* for the accomplishment of those ends.

Of course CEOs should have a job description, but not one written by the board. The CEO should write his or her own. The CEO then uses that job description as a tool to guide subordinates in preparing their own job descriptions.

That job description should be a statement of:

- the job's purpose,
- the tasks to be achieved by the individual, measurable in time and quantity,
- organizational relationships, and
- the training and development projected for better performance of the job.

This is therefore Clearly a Management Tool

The board is certainly concerned with the performance of the CEO. However, the board's concern is with what the CEO is accomplishing through the entire organization, not day-to-day accomplishments.

A board needs to be very clear with the CEO regarding its expectations for the organization. These expectations should be specific and in written form and should clearly indicate how the board will evaluate the CEO's performance in leading the organization toward its goals.

There are at least four reasons why boards cannot effectively do CEO job descriptions:

1. It would require that boards be prescriptive regarding *means* rather than being proscriptive. That is, the board states positively what the organization will accomplish but states negatively what the staff may not do with regard to means.

2. Governance by its very nature precludes the measuring of activities. Governance is concerned only with:

   - the ends for which the organization exists;

   - the executive limitations stating negatively what the staff may not do in the pursuit of those ends;

   - board/staff linkage where the board states clearly how it passes authority to the staff and how it will perform its assessment of result; and

   - board process wherein the board puts in writing its own rules for how it performs board work.

3. Job descriptions require one-on-one measurement, coaching, and course correcting. Obviously, boards should not attempt this kind of involvement with activities. Boards are too far removed from the action to perform this kind of work.

4. Job descriptions are dynamic, never static. They need to be continually updated by the jobholder to adapt to ever-changing conditions and demands within the organization.

And finally, job descriptions are task-oriented for the individual, not group-oriented for the achievement of organizational ends.

There is no more delicate and symbiotic relationship in management than that of the board with the CEO. When these two forces clash, the result is often debilitating frustration.

The most frequently applied antidote is for the board to write the CEO's job description.

There is hope. Ensure that the board addresses the ends for which the organization exists, and that the leader knows that his or her primary task is to progress toward the accomplishment of those ends and then leave the means for the pursuing of those ends to the CEO.

The Perils of Executive Appraisal

My young friend sat across the table from me in the coffee shop. He was perplexed to know how to respond to the board's executive appraisal recently completed. I knew him well. I had served him and his organization as management consultant two years earlier. He is one of the brightest and most competent young leaders I have met.

The appraisal process used by the board was typical but ineffective. One of the board members had been designated to compile the results of a survey sent to both board and staff. Then the same individual was assigned the task of meeting with the young man to disclose the results. The staff scored him a low 5, on a scale of 1 to 5, while the board gave him a high 3. When my friend asked for specifics, he was given such vague observations as, "You travel too much," "You are too aloof," and the like.

I have never known this capable leader to be defensive. He is always eager to learn. Now, he finds himself being battered by information, which hurts but does not help.

In my career, I have never known of or read of an executive appraisal that was done well. We would be better off to abandon the process than to do it poorly. However, there is a way to do it that will both benefit the organization and the executive.

There is a symbiotic relationship between the board and the CEO of a ministry. A board without a CEO is an empty shell. A CEO without a board is vulnerable. Both need each other. Just as it is vital that board/CEO operational roles are clear, so it is with regard to the evaluation process. It may well be that the obfuscation of roles in operations contributes most to the muddled appraisal process. When boards dabble in operations, telling staff what to do, it is easy for the evaluation process to result in looking at what the CEO is *doing* rather than measuring what he and his team are *accomplishing*.

The first step in executive appraisal is mutually agreed-upon standards in written form, measurable in quantity and time. Earl Nightingale once said that human beings don't have trouble achieving goals, just setting them. How true! But if it is difficult to set goals for oneself, how much more so for a board and an individual CEO to determine executive measurement standards.

The question then naturally arises as to who initiates the writing of these measurements. In an ideal world an ideal board would sit around a table and produce the appraisal criteria. However, in reality it is probably the CEO who brings the board the first draft.

What is important is not who puts words on paper first, but that the board comes to moral ownership of the standards. Then there is some hope that the board will hold the CEO to his commitments.

Executive appraisal must result from a process of interim monitoring by means of reports. The board owes it to the CEO to be very specific as to what information it wants on an interim basis. The CEO owes it to the board to faithfully provide that information. This tactic alone will remove many of the surprises and subjectivity from the evaluation once it actually takes place. The CEO preparing his progress reports will know first himself how he is doing, even before he makes out his reports.

In the example of my young friend in the coffee shop, the board had designated an individual to meet with him to convey its findings. Big mistake! If a board is to perform executive appraisal, the whole group should participate. The board in its entirety must bear this responsibility. There are some tasks that can never be delegated.

A word needs to be said about asking the staff to evaluate its boss. There is an old management adage that says that no one should be subordinate to and a critic of another at the same time. The board's task is to measure accomplishment, not popularity. A successful CEO will always have detractors. If he has enough of them it will be reflected in his failure to attain the goals he has set. Louis A. Allen used to say that leaders should never be upset by moderate grousing. Likewise, boards must be willing to endure some staff dissatisfaction with a CEO. If the board wants a CEO to have no critics, it is being unreasonable.

All of this really comes down to expectations. A board may have a set of expectations never understood by the CEO. In time, frustration gives way to tension, and then to conflict. By then it is usually too late to conduct an executive appraisal. Board members begin muttering about how to get rid of the individual. Or, people begin resigning from the board.

I am often asked about performance appraisal forms. Through the years I have reviewed scores of such instruments. I have even used them. I wish I hadn't, and I refuse to now. They are worthless! These forms are crutches that boards use to avoid the hard work of putting in writing the criteria by which they will evaluate the performance of an individual.

Finally, a few guidelines:

- Begin with written, measurable organizational ends, mutually agreed-upon by board and CEO.

- Specify interim reporting processes; insure objectivity and avoid subjectivity.
- Measure results, not activities.
- Require full board participation.
- If you can't do the above, abandon the process!

Boards and Fund Raising

There is no more recurring question in the non-profit organization than the role of the board in fund raising. This single issue has prompted the resignation of board members as well as staff in countless instances. Why this confusion and frustration? What can be done to clarify roles and expectations?

The starting point is the thinking that precedes the invitation to serve on a board. We hear of someone of means who shares the values of our ministry and immediately think we should ask him or her to join our board. This often happens with little or no introduction, written expectations, or orientation. After all, he has money and likes what we are doing. Or we conclude that a segment of the population needs to be represented on our board and cast about for a likely prospect. More, much more than this is involved if we are to avoid conflict in the future.

Donors first — No one should ever be asked to serve on a non-profit board unless they are already giving to the organization. This alone will ensure that there is already a commitment to and at least some understanding of the work. My friend John Pearson says he never invites anyone to join the board of CMA unless he or she is already giving to CMA. This one strategy will avoid many problems.

Expectations in writing — You have heard that a verbal agreement is not worth the paper it is written on. True. If a matter can be misunderstood, it will be misunderstood. It is not uncommon to have board members sign a doctrinal statement. Why not also have a signed statement regarding giving, board conduct, and attendance? Some of my clients call this a covenant.

The leader of an organization called me to ask my opinion of having his board members agree to give $10,000 each year to remain on his board. I urged him not to proceed. That is a bad idea prior to becoming a member and a potentially disastrous step after the fact. For the person who is unable to give that amount it is an embarrassment. For the person who can give more it is an insult. The fact of giving should be a condition for membership. The amount should be solely the decision of the individual. To be sure, there are times when we should ask an individual for a specific amount. This should be based on the relationship to the person and knowledge of his or her giving history and ability to give.

The board and development strategy — Only theology boasts more experts than development. When I was in seminary I served a very small church in the mountains of Tennessee. Never have I witnessed more provincialism and ignorance. Yet the old men who sat around the pot-bellied stove in the country store fancied themselves experts in theology. Similar arrogance takes place in board meetings when discussing development.

Kathleen Kelly says categorically in her new book, *Effective Fund-Raising Management*, that development is a science. There is an age-old debate, especially in Christian circles, as to whether development is an art or a science. This is precipitated in part because of the relationship of the Holy Spirit and prayer to the whole process of raising money for God's work. Development, like everything else in ministry, should be subject to the Spirit's guidance and prayer but should not deter us from pursuing the knowledge required by this science. Of course development is an art. How human beings relate to one another is an art. Fund raising is dependent on relationships. That does not make it any less a science. Most development efforts fail due to a lack of the science of development rather than a deficiency in relationships.

You may well have a board member who is expert in some aspect of development. It is not uncommon to find board people who know publications, computers, graphic design, or some other discipline vital to fund raising. We should draw upon that specialty, obviously. But we should do so as individuals, not as board members, keeping in mind that the most valuable help might come from someone outside the board.

The board network — When people are invited to serve on a board, it should be clearly understood that you expect them to introduce your development specialists to their acquaintances for donor cultivation. Board people who may be terrified at the thought of asking for a gift will almost always be willing to introduce you so that you can ask. Whenever possible have the board member accompany you on the call. All of us know of the value of this tactic in training for evangelism. Why not use it in development with the hope that at least some people will conclude they can eventually do the same work on their own? Being unwilling to do this should disqualify them from serving on the board.

Bibliography

Alexander, John W. *Managing Our Work*. Downers Grove, IL: InterVaristy Press, 1975.

Allen, Louis A. *Management and Organization*. New York, NY: McGraw-Hill, 1958.

---------. *The Management Profession*. New York, NY: McGraw-Hill, 1964.

Andringa & Engstrom. *Nonprofit Board Answer Book*. Washington, D.C.: NCNB Books, 1997.

Appley, Lawrence. *Management in Action*. New York, NY: AMA, 1956.

Barna, George. *The Power of Vision*. Ventura, CA: Regal Books, 1992.

Beatty, Jack. *The World According to Peter Drucker*. New York, NY: The Free Press, 1998.

Belasco, James A. *Teaching the Elephant to Dance*. London: Random House UK Ltd., Century Business Press, 1990.

Bennis, Warren. *Why Leaders Can't Lead*. San Francisco, CA: Jossey-Bass, 1997.

Bennis, Warren, and Burt Nanus. *Leaders: The Stategies for Taking Charge*. New York, NY: Harper and Row, 1985.

Biehl & Engstrom. *Boardroom Confidence*. Sisters, OR: Questar Publishers, 1988.

Biehl, Bobb. *Increasing Your Leadership Confidence*. Sisters, OR: Questar Publishers, 1989.

---------. *Master-Planning*. Nashville, TN: Broadman and Holman Publishers, 1997.

Bruce, A. B. *The Training of the Twelve*. Grand Rapids, MI: Kriegel Publications, 1968.

Burns and Stalker. *The Managment of Innovation*. New York, NY: Oxford University Press, 1994.

Callahan, Kennon L. *Effective Church Leadership.* San Francisco, CA: Jossey-Bass, 1997.

---------. *Giving and Stewardship in an Effective Church.* San Francisco, CA: Harper Publishing, 1992.

Carlson, Dick. *Delegation.*

Carver, John. *Boards That Make a Difference.* San Francisco, CA: Jossey-Bass Publishers, 1990.

---------. *A New Vision of Board Leadership.* Washington, D.C.: Association of Community College Trustees, 1994.

---------. *Reinventing Your Board.* San Francisco, CA: Jossey-Bass Publishers, 1997.

Chait, Richard P. *How to Help Your Board Govern More and Manage Less.* Washington, D.C.: National Center for Nonprofit Boards, 1993.

Clinton, J. Robert. *The Making of a Leader.* Colorado Springs, CO: Navpress, 1988.

Collins & Porras. *Built to Last.* New York, NY: Harper Business, 1994.

Cousins, Don, Leith Anderson, and Arthur DeKruyter. *Mastering Church Management.* Portland, OR: Multnomah Press, 1990.

Covey, Stephen R. *First Things First.* New York, NY: Simon & Schuster, 1994.

---------. *Principal Centered Leadership.* New York, NY: Summit Books, 1991.

---------. *The Seven Habits of Highly Effective People.* New York, NY: Simon & Schuster, 1989.

Damazio, Frank. *The Making of a Leader.* Portland, OR: Bible Temple Publishing, 1988.

Davis, Ken. *Secrets of Dynamic Communication.* Grand Rapids, MI: Zondervan Publishing House, 1991.

DePree, Max. *Leadership Is an Art.* New York, NY: Doubleday, 1989.

---------. *Leadership Jazz.* New York, NY: Dell Publishing, 1992.

---------. *Leading Without Power.* San Francisco, CA: Jossey-Bass Publishers, 1997.

Drucker, Peter S. *Adventures of a Bystander.* New York, NY: Harper & Row, 1978.

---------. *The Age of Discontinuity.* New York, NY: Harper & Row, 1968.

---------. *The Changing World of the Executive.* New York, NY: Truman Talley Books, 1982.

---------. *Concept of the Corporation.* New York, NY: New American Library, 1946.

---------. *The Effective Executive.* New York, NY: Harper & Row, 1966.

---------. *The Frontiers of Management.* New York, NY: Truman Talley Books,

1986.

---------. *The Future of Industrial Man.* New York, NY: New American Library, 1942.

---------. *Management Challenges for the 21st Century.* New York, NY: Harper Business, 1999.

---------. *Managing for Results.* New York, NY: Harper & Row, 1964.

---------. *Managing in a Time of Great Change.* New York, NY: Truman, Talley Books/Dutton, 1995.

---------. *Managing in Turbulent Times.* New York, NY: Harper & Row, 1980.

---------. *Managing the Nonprofit Organization.* New York, NY: Harper & Row, 1990.

---------. *Men, Ideas and Politics.* New York, NY: Harper & Row, 1971.

---------. *The New Realities.* New York, NY: Harper & Row, 1989.

---------. *The New Society.* New York, NY: Harper & Row, 1949.

---------. *On the Profession of Management.* Boston, MA: Harvard Business Review Books, 1998.

---------. *Toward the Next Economics.* New York, NY: Harper & Row, 1981.

Engstrom, Ted W. *The Making of a Christian Leader.* Grand Rapids, MI: Zondervan, 1976.

Farson, Richard. *Management of the Absurd.* New York, NY: Simon & Schuster, 1996.

Fisher & Sharp. *Getting It Done.* New York, NY: Harper Business, 1998.

Finzel, Hans. *Top Ten Mistakes Leaders Make.* Wheaton, IL: Victor Books, 1994.

Ford, Leighton. *Transforming Leadership.* Downers Grove, IL: InterVarsity Press, 1991.

Gangel, Kenneth O. *Feeding and Leading.* Wheaton, IL: Victor Books, 1989.

---------. *Team Leadership in Christian Ministry.* Chicago, IL: Moody Press, 1997.

Gardner, John W. *On Leadership.* New York, NY: The Free Press, 1990.

Garfield, Charles. *Second to None.* Homewood, IL: Business One Irwin, 1992.

Gerber, Michael E. *The E-Myth Manager.* New York, NY: Harper Business, 1998.

Greenfield, James M. *Fund Raising Fundamentals.* New York, NY: John Wylie & Sons, 1994.

Greenleaf, Robert K. *On Becoming a Servant Leader.* San Francisco, CA: Jossey-Bass Publishers, 1996.

---------. *The Servant as Religious Leader.* Indianapolis, IN: The Robert K. Greenleaf Center, 1982.

----------. *Servant Leadership*. New York, NY: Paulist Press, 1977.

----------. *Spirituality as Leadership*. Indianapolis, IN: The Robert K. Greenleaf Center, 1988.

----------. *Trustees as Servants*. Indianapolis, IN: The Robert K. Greenleaf Center, 1990.

Habecker, Eugene B. *Rediscovering the Soul of Leadership*. Wheaton, IL: Victor Books, 1996.

Harvey, Jerry B. *The Abilene Paradox*. San Francisco, CA: Jossey-Bass Publishers, 1998.

Hayward, Steven F. *Churchill on Leadership*. Rockland, CA: Forum Publications, 1997.

Herman, Robert D. & Associates. *The Jossey-Bass Handbook of Nonprofit Leadership and Management*. San Francisco, CA: Jossey-Bass Publishers, 1994.

Hesselbein, Goldsmith, and Beckhard. *The Leader of the Future*. San Francisco, CA: Jossey-Bass Publishers, 1996.

----------. *The Organization of the Future*. San Francisco, CA: Jossey-Bass Publishers, 1997.

Hirzy, Ellen Cochran. *Nonprofit Board Committees*. Washington, D.C.: National Center for Nonprofit Boards, 1993.

Howe, Fisher. *The Boardmembers Guide to Fund Raising*. San Francisco, CA: Jossey-Bass Publishers, 1991.

Kelly, Kathleen S. *Effective Fund-Raising Management*. Mahwah, NJ: Lawrence Erlbaum Associates, Publishers, 1998.

Kets De Vries. *Manfred F. R. Leaders, Fools and Imposters*. San Francisco, CA: 1993.

Knudsen, Raymond B. *Stewardship Enlistment and Commitment*. Wilton, CT: Morehouse-Barlow, 1985.

Kotter, John P. *A Force for Change*. New York, NY: The Free Press, 1990.

----------. *Leading Change*. Boston, MA: Harvard Business School Press, 1996.

Koontz, Harold, and Heinz Weihrich. *Essentials of Management*. New York, NY: McGraw Hill Publishing, 1990.

Kouzes, James, and Barry Posner. *Credibility*. San Francisco, CA: Jossey-Bass Publishers, 1997.

----------. *The Leadership Challenge*. San Francisco, CA: Jossey-Bass Publishers, 1995.

Lant, Dr. Jeffrey. *Development Today*. Cambridge, MA: JLA Publications, 1980.

Maxwell, John C. *Developing the Leaders Around You*. Nashville, TN: Thomas Nelson Publishers, 1995.

----------. *Developing the Leader Within You*. Nashville, TN: Thomas Nelson

Publishers, 1993.

----------. *The 21 Indinspensable Qualities of a Leader.* Nashville, TN: Thomas Nelson Publishers, 1999.

McIntosh & Rima. *Overcoming the Dark Side of Leadership.* Grand Rapids, MI: Baker Books, 1997.

McLeish, Barry J. *Successful Marketing Strategies for Nonprofit Organizations.* New York, NY: John Wiley & Sons, 1995.

McNeal, Reggie. *Revolution in Leadership.* Nashville, TN: Abingdon Press, 1998.

Miller, Calvin. *The Empowered Leader.* Nashville: Broadman & Holman Publishers, 1995.

Mixer, Joseph R. *Principles of Professional Fund Raising.* San Francisco, CA: Jossey-Bass Publishers, 1993.

Mueller, Robert K. *Smarter Board Meetings: For Effective Nonprofit Governance.* Washington, D.C.: National Center for Nonprofit Boards, 1992.

Osbourne, Alex. *Applied Imagination.* New York, NY: Scribner's, 1963.

Orr, Robert A. *The Essentials for Effective Leadership Development.* Linden, Alberta, Canada: Leadership Essentials Press, 1994.

Pollard, Willam C. *The Soul of the Firm.* Grand Rapids, MI: Zondervan Publishing, 1996.

Powell, James Lawrence. *Pathways to Leadership.* San Francisco, CA: Jossey-Bass Publishing, 1995.

Rosso, Henry A. *Rosso on Fundraising.* San Francisco, CA: Jossey-Bass Publishing, 1996.

Saffold, Guy S. *Strategic Planning for Christian Organizations.* Fayetteville, AR: Accrediting Association of Bible Colleges, 1994.

Sanders, J. Oswald. *Spiritual Leadership.* Chicago, IL: Moody Press, 1994.

Schaller, Lyle E. *The Change Agent.* Nashville, TN: Abingdon Press, 1972.

----------. *Forty-four Ways to Expand the Financial Base of Your Congregation.* Nashville, TN: Abingdon Press, 1989.

Senge, Peter, M. *The Fifth Discipline.* New York, NY: Doubleday Currency, 1990.

Shaw, Robert Bruce. *Trust in the Balance.* San Francisco, CA: Jossey-Bass, 1997.

Spears, Larry C. *Reflections on Leadership.* New York, NY: John Wiley & Sons, 1995.

Stoesz, Edgar. *Doing Good Better.* Intercourse, PA: Good Books, 1994.

Stoner, James, and Edward Freeman. *Management.* Englewood Cliffs, NJ: Prentice Hall, 1992.

Stowell, Joseph M. *Shepherding the Church*. Chicago, IL: Moody Press, 1997.

Swindoll, Charles. *Hand Me Another Brick*. New York, NY: Bantam Books, 1983.

Tarrant, John J. *Drucker: The Man Who Invented the Corporate Society*. Boston, MA: Cahners Books, 1976.

Weiss, Alan. *Our Emperors Have No Clothes*. Franklin Lakes, NJ: Career Press, 1995.

Werning, Waldo J. *Christian Stewards Confronted and Committed*. St. Louis, MO: Concordia Publishing House, 1982.

White, John. *Excellence in Leadership*. Downers Grove, IL: InterVarisity, 1986.

Wren, J. Thomas, ed. *The Leader's Companion*. New York, NY: The Free Press, 1995.

Young, Hollister, and Hodgkinson. *Governing, Leading, and Managing Nonprofit Organizations*. San Francisco, CA: Jossey-Bass Publishers, 1993.

Zander, Alvin. *Making Boards Effective*. San Francisco, CA: Jossey-Bass Publishers, 1993.

Endnotes

Chapter 1
    1. Engstrom, The Making of a Christian Leader, p. 25.

Chapter 2
    1. Burns and Stallker, The Management of Innovation.
    2. Greenleaf, Servant Leadership, pp.13-14.
    3. Depree, Leadership Jazz, pp. 220-224.

Chapter 4
    1. Kouzes and Posner, The Leadership Challenge, p. 27.
    2. Gardner, On Leadership, p. 1.

Chapter 5
    1. Bennis and Nanus, Leaders: The Strategies for Taking Charge, p. 37.
    2. Depree, Leadership Is an Art, p. 3.
    3. Gangel, Feeding and Leading, p. 14.

Chapter 7
    1. Appley, Management in Action, p. 26.

Chapter 9
    1. Bennis and Nanus, Leaders: The Strategies for Taking Charge.

Chapter 10
    1. Bennis and Nanus, Leaders: The Strategies for Taking Charge.

Chapter 11
    1. Carlson, Delegation.

Chapter 14
    1. Carver, Boards That Make a Difference, p. 17.
    2. Weiss, Our Emperors Have No Clothes, p. 40.
    3. Osbourne, Applied Imagination.

Other Exciting Products from ChurchSmart Resources

Natural Church Development

By Christian Schwarz

In an attempt to put denominational and cultural distinctives aside, the author has researched 1000 churches in 32 countries to determine the quality characteristics that growing, healthy churches share. Schwarz's research indicates that quality churches score high in eight quality characteristics, but will only grow to the level that their minimum factor (or lowest of these eight characteristics) will allow them. This book is a must read!
ChurchSmart price $19.95

Raising Leaders for the Harvest

By Robert Logan & Neil Cole

Raising Leaders for the Harvest introduces the concept of Leadership Farm Systems, an organic process of leadership development which results in natural and spontaneous multiplication of disciples, groups, ministries and churches. This resource kit includes six audio cassettes and an action planning guide with worksheets. Discover how to raise leaders in your church for the harvest in your community!
ChurchSmart price $60.00

Focused Living Resource Kit

By Terry Walling

Focused Living is a personal development process designed to help believers bring strategic focus to their life and ministry. Focus is obtained by examining their past (Perspective — Personal Time-Line), clarifying their future (Focus — Personal Mission Statement) and identifying resources that will facilitate future growth and effectiveness (Mentoring — Personal Mentors). This resource includes six audio cassettes, three self-discovery workbooks and a leader's guide.
ChurchSmart price $60.00